AF575483

# PRISMS

# PRISMS

E. A. Seguy

DOVER PUBLICATIONS, INC.
Mineola, New York

*Bibliographical Note*

*Prisms*, first published by Dover Publications, Inc., in 2016, is an unabridged republication, in English, of Seguy's portfolio *40 Planches de Dessins et Coloris Nouveaux*, originally published by Editions d'Art Charles Moreau, Paris, in 1931.

*Library of Congress Cataloging-in-Publication Data*

Names: Séguy, E. A. (Emile-Allain), 1877–1951, artist.
Title: Prisms / E.A. Seguy.
Other titles: Prismes
Description: Mineola, New York : Dover Publications, 2016. | "Prisms, first published by Dover Publications, Inc., in 2016, is an unabridged republication, in English, of Seguy's portfolio 40 Planches de Dessins et Coloris Nouveaux, originally published by Editions d'Art Charles Moreau, Paris, in 1931."
Identifiers: LCCN 2016022574 | ISBN 9780486810119 (paperback) | ISBN 0486810119
Subjects: LCSH: Séguy, E. A. (Emile-Allain), 1877–1951—Themes, motives. | BISAC: ART / History / Modern (late 19th Century to 1945). | ART / European.
Classification: LCC NE2240.6.S44 A4 2016 | DDC 700.92—dc23 LC record available at https://lccn.loc.gov/2016022574

Manufactured in the United States
81011901 2016
www.doverpublications.com

# Publisher's Note

This book reproduces all forty plates from the rare E. A. Seguy pochoir portfolio *Prismes*, published in 1931 in Paris by Editions d'Art Charles Moreau. As the last of the approximately one dozen magnificent design portfolios created by the French graphic artist E. A. Seguy during the first thirty years of the twentieth century, it represents the culmination of one of the most elusive and unusual careers in the history of twentieth-century graphic art.

Unlike many other such valedictory volumes, however, *Prismes* does not look back at Seguy's long career in the interest of reviewing any of his work which had gone before. Though coming after thirty years of great productivity, the portfolio's most striking quality is that it represents a new departure for Seguy. Gone, but certainly not forgotten, are the magnificent Art Nouveau colors and graphic style which informed his earliest, largely floral pochoir plates from before World War I. Not referred to either are the equally magnificent portfolios of fantastic butterflies and other insects from the 1920s. The designs in *Prismes* are new, not based on botanical forms and flowers, but using geometric and futuristic shapes and also, to a large extent, a new color palette for Seguy. *Prismes* made explicit the way in which Seguy became one of the rare graphic artists who managed to transition seamlessly from Art Nouveau to Art Deco.

Where Seguy went after *Prismes,* no one can say. It is Seguy's final statement, and it isn't known where or how much longer he lived or what he did next after it was finished and published. The original colorful and intriguing plates from *Prismes* are often sold individually these days from copies of the very rare portfolio broken up for that purpose, so the reader of this volume now has the opportunity to own and enjoy representations of all forty of these energetic and intensely modern decorative plates. The pochoir technique, using stencils to apply layers of deep color, was always ideally suited to Seguy's vision and style, regardless of how it evolved over the decades following his 1902 portfolio, *Les fleurs et leurs applications décoratives* (Flowers and Their Decorative Applications). If the plants and flowers, and the butterflies and insects of the earlier years, represent the height of what Seguy accomplished as a graphic artist, the plates reproduced here are certainly a starting point for the continued investigation of a remarkable and still to be fully explored career.

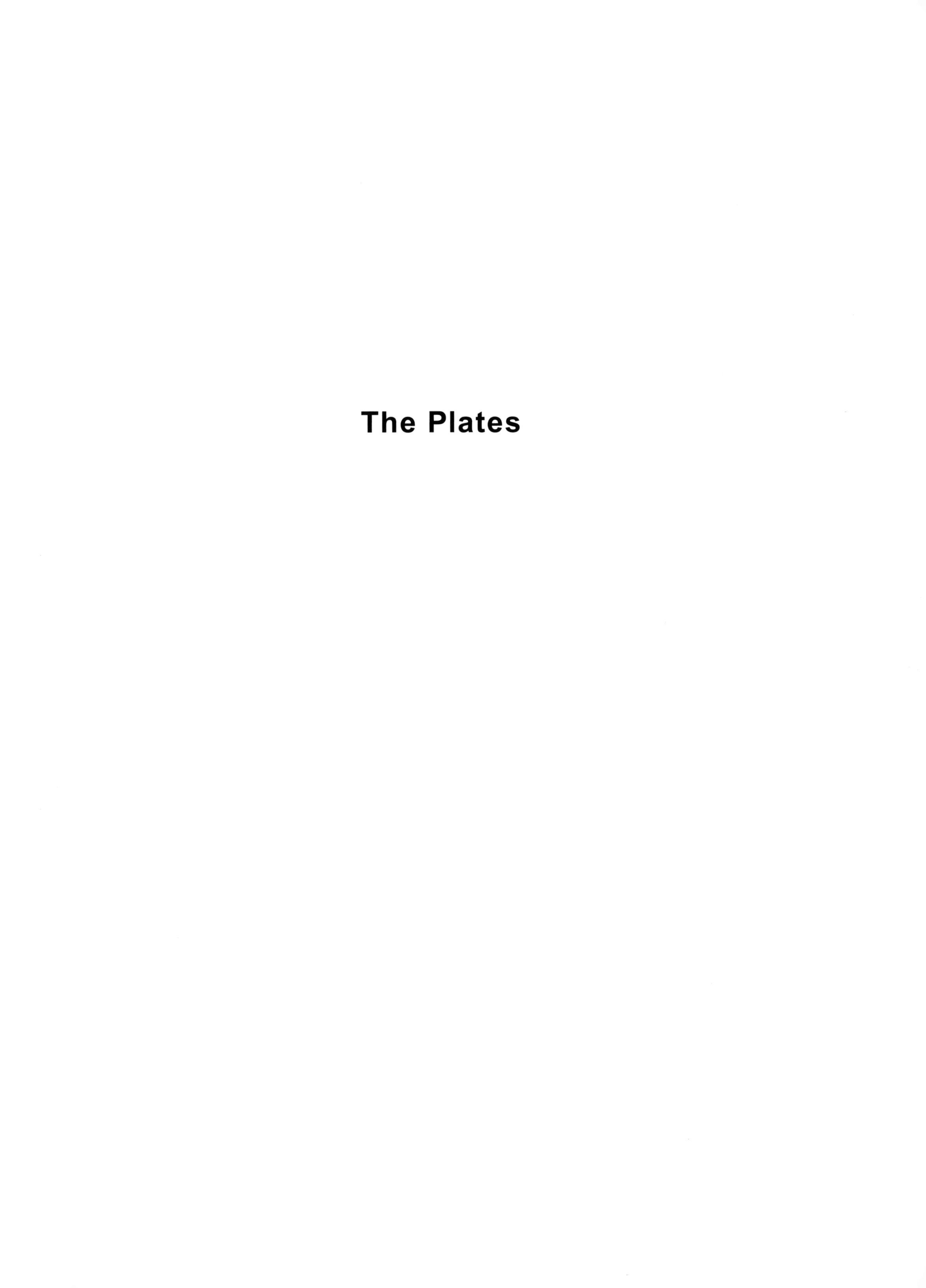

# The Plates

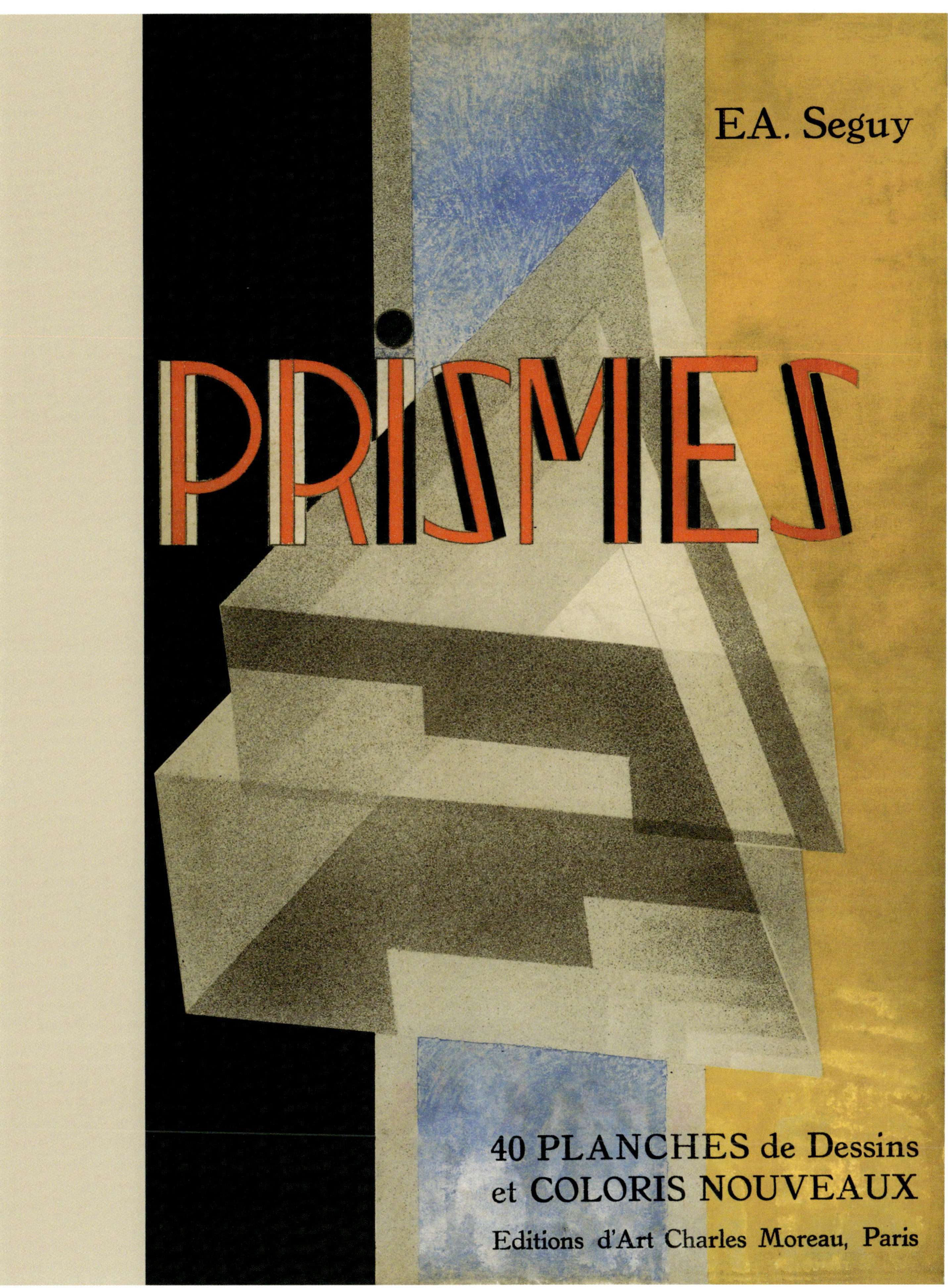


Original Cover

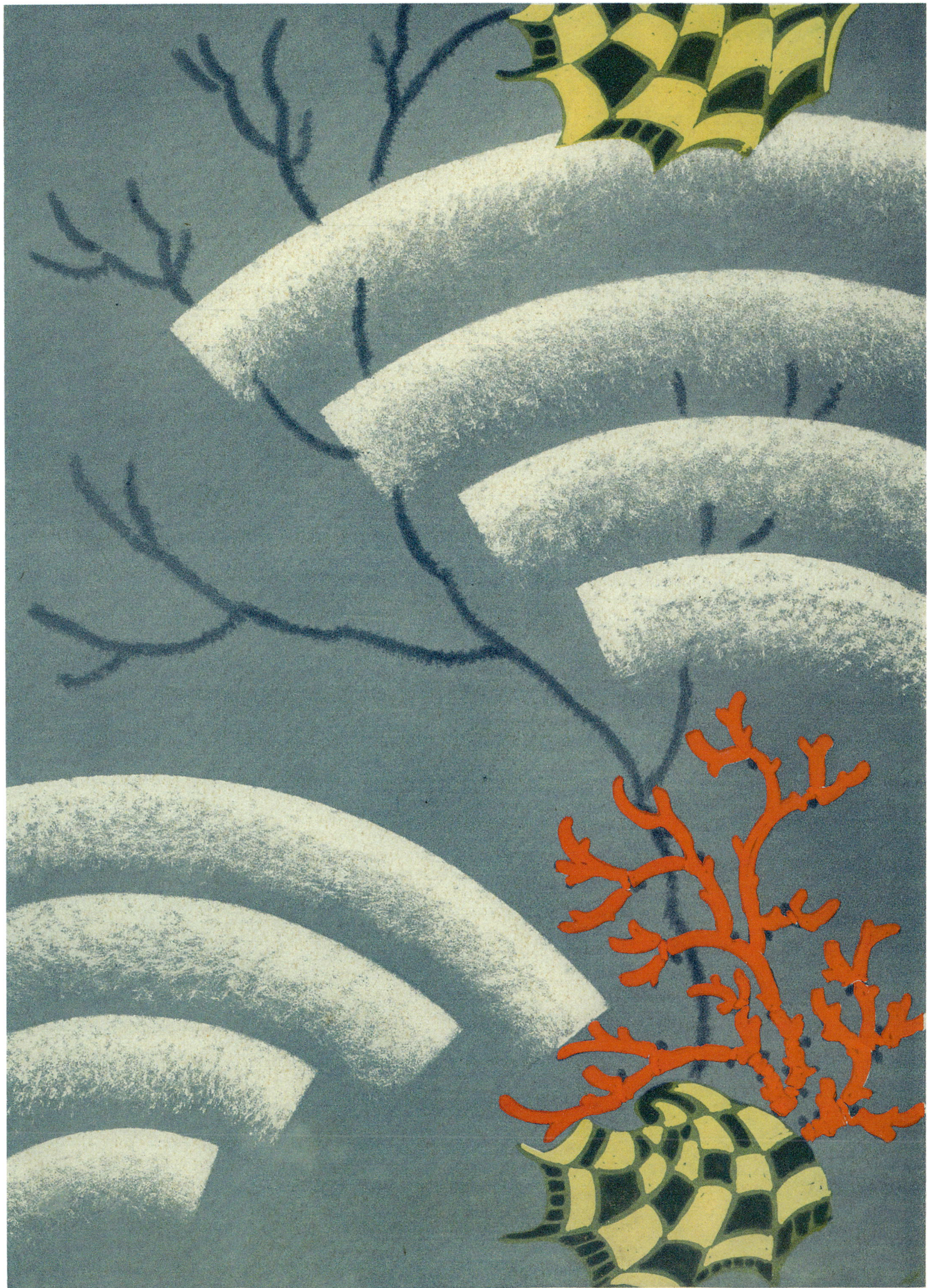

Plate 1

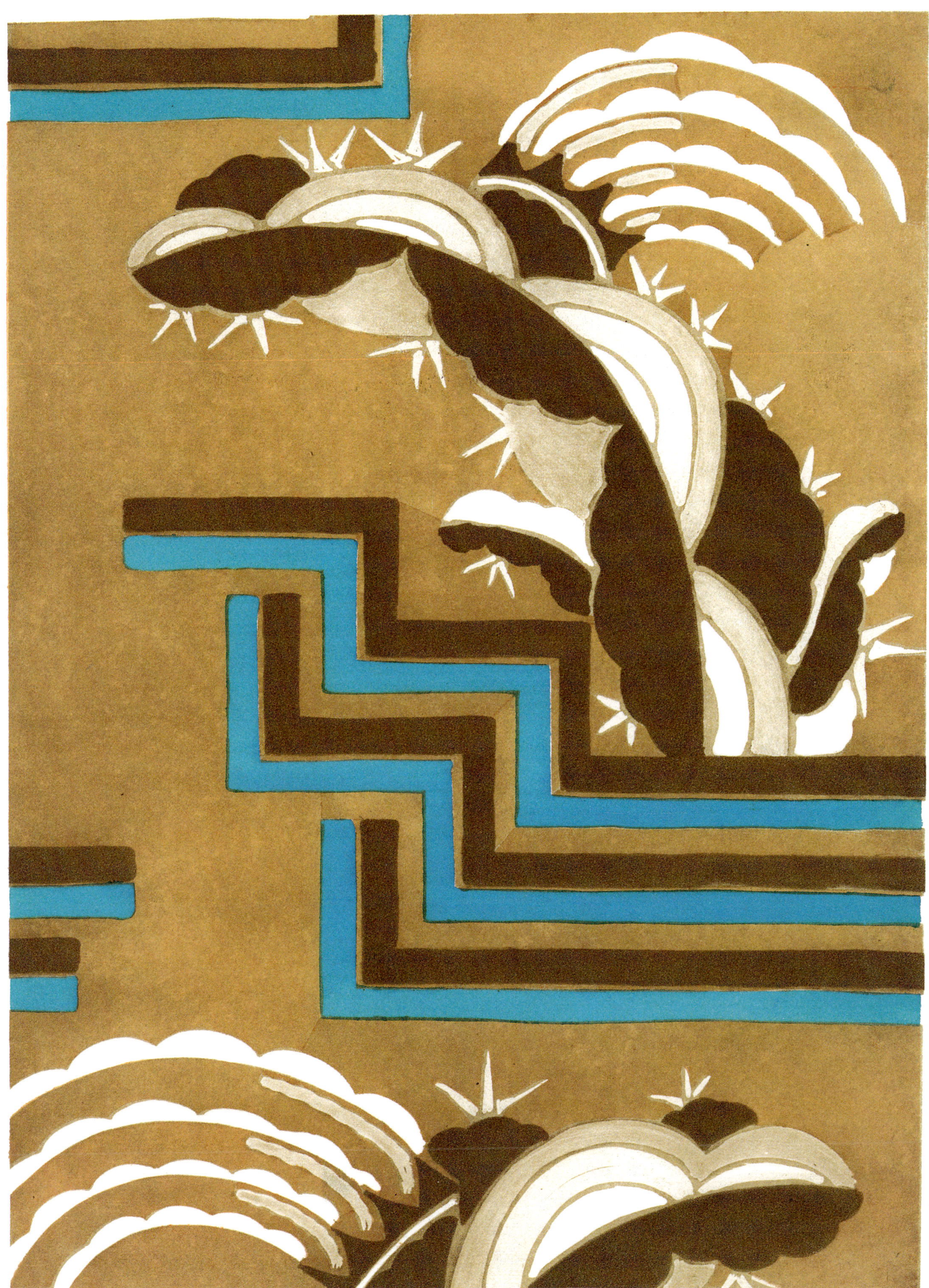

Plate 2

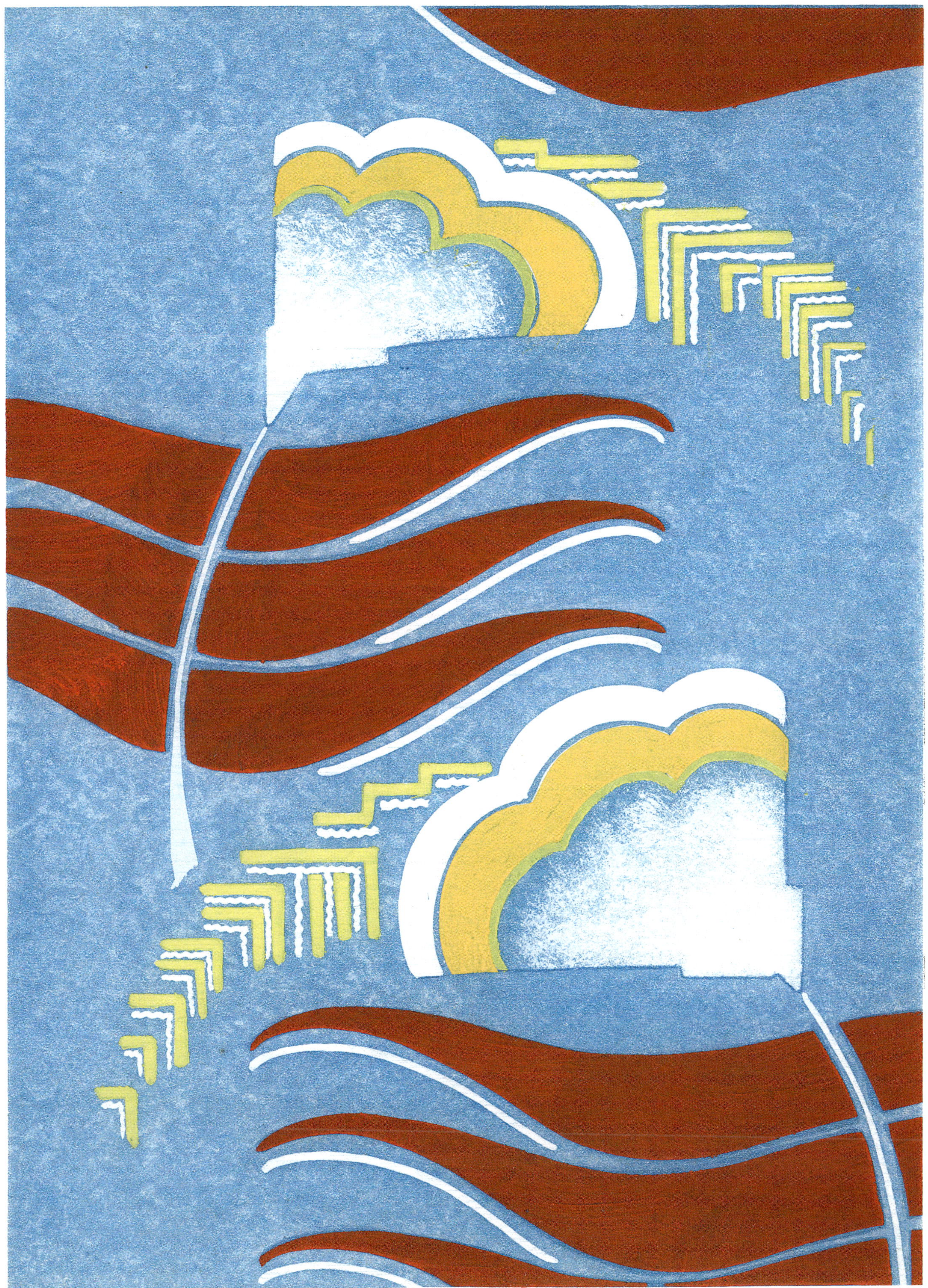

Plate 3

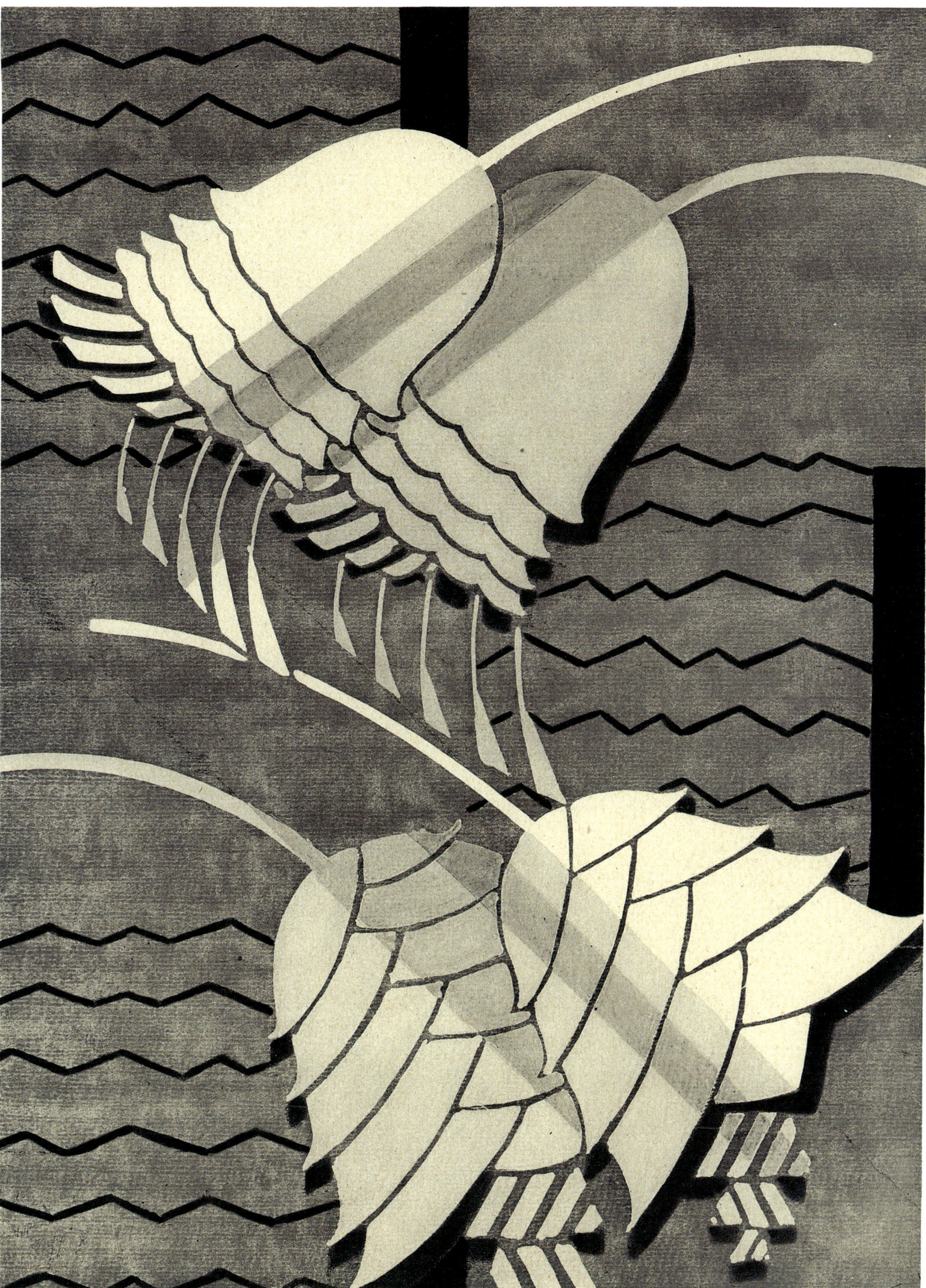

Plate 4

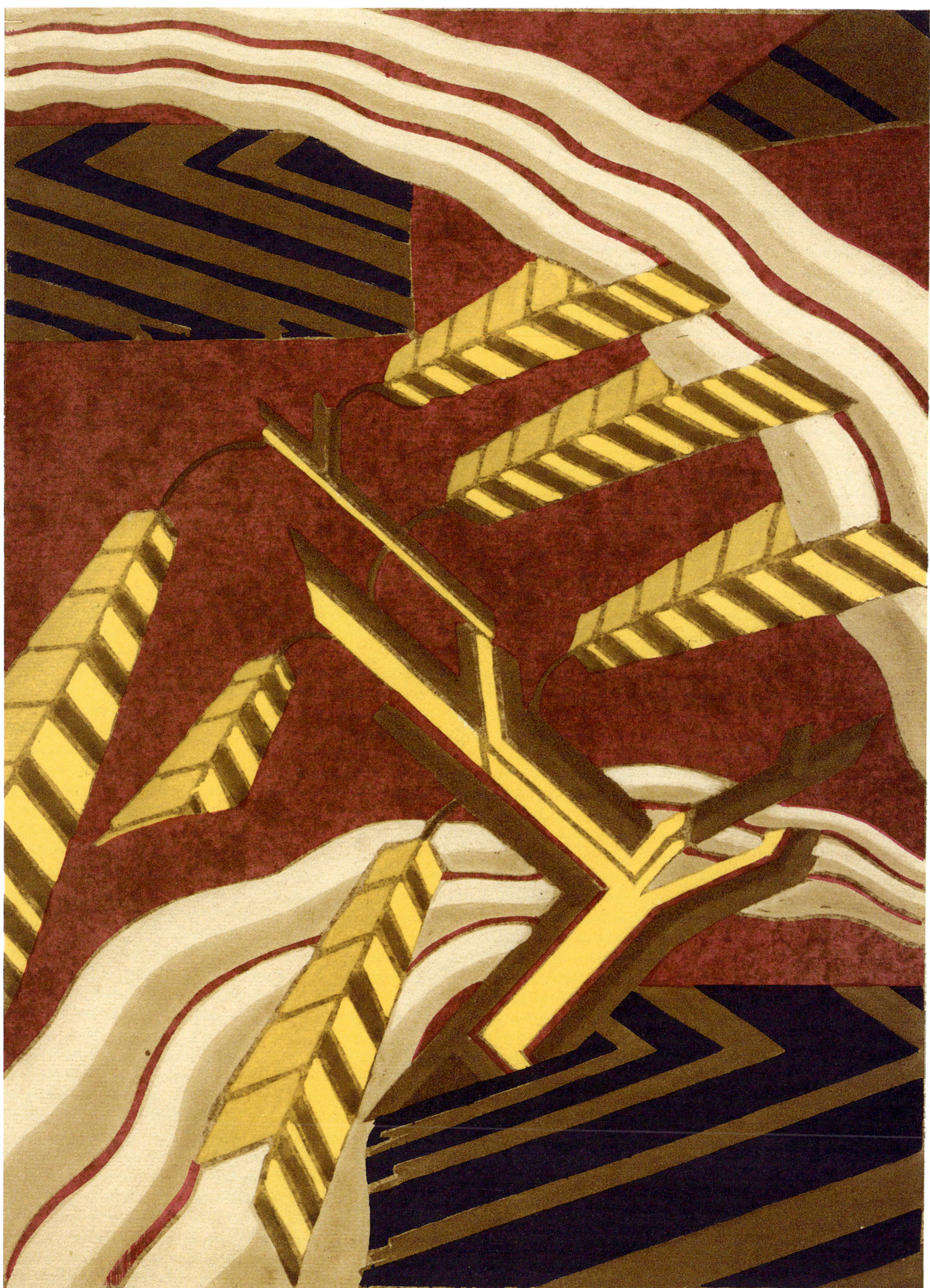

Plate 5

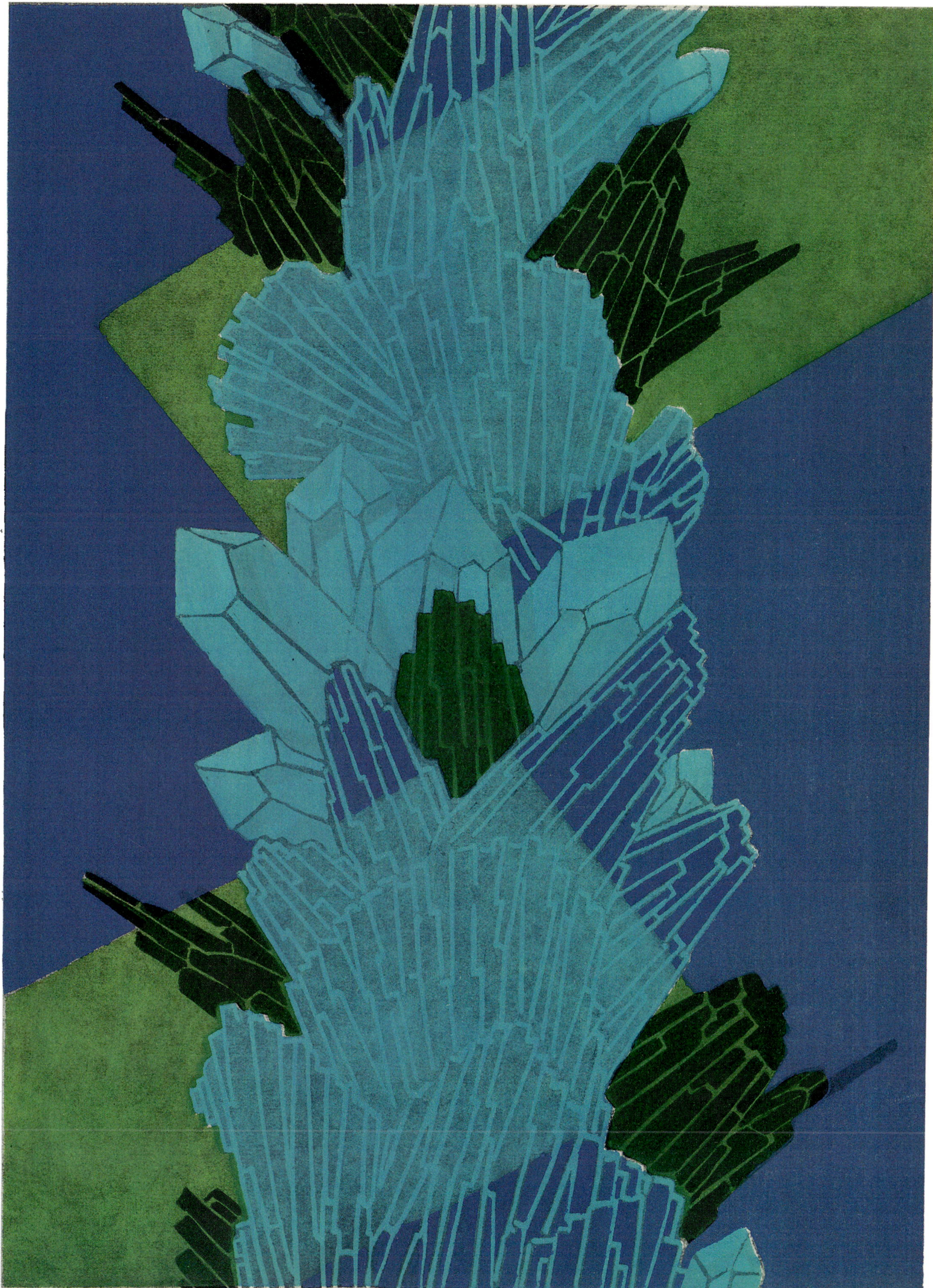

Plate 6

Plate 7

Plate 8

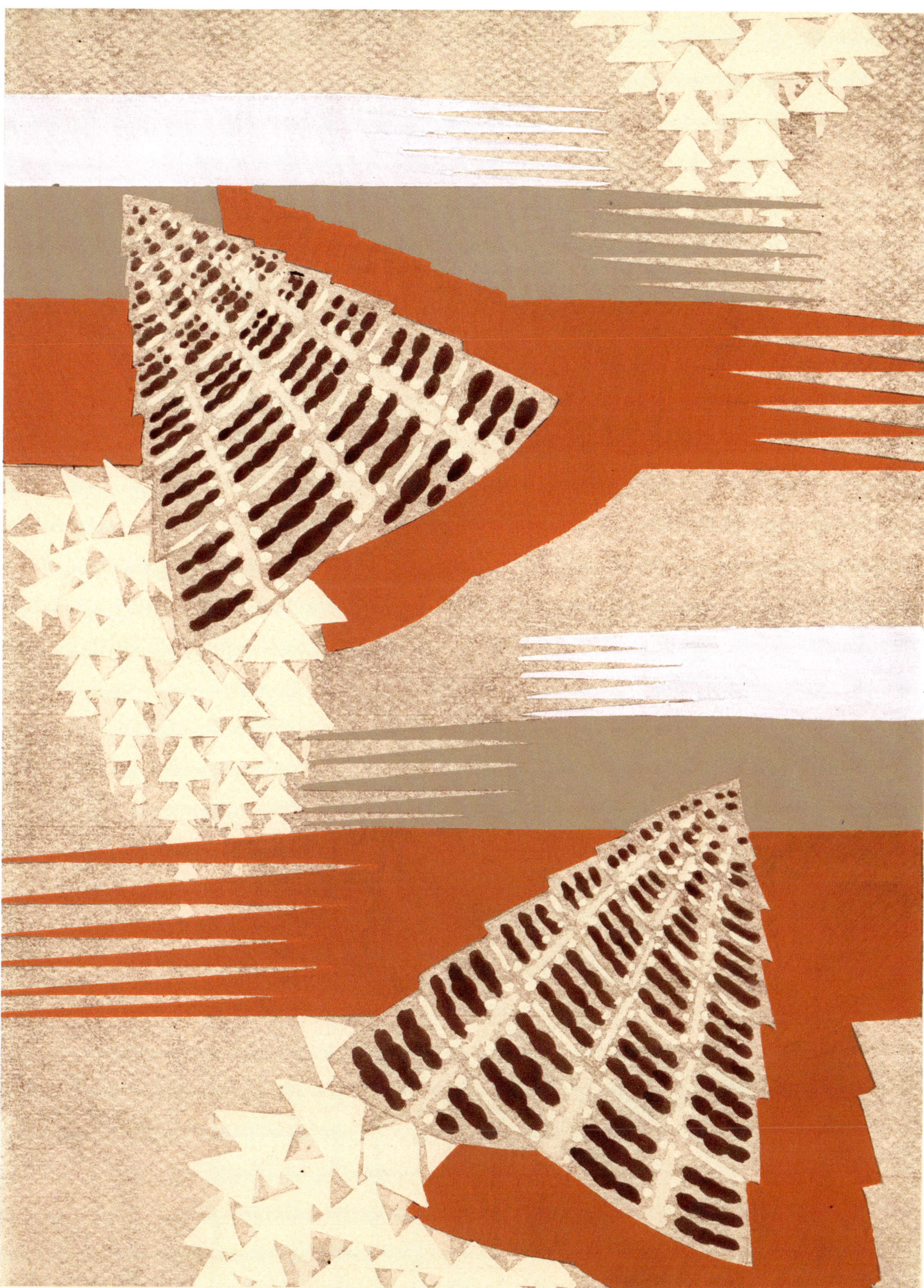

Plate 9

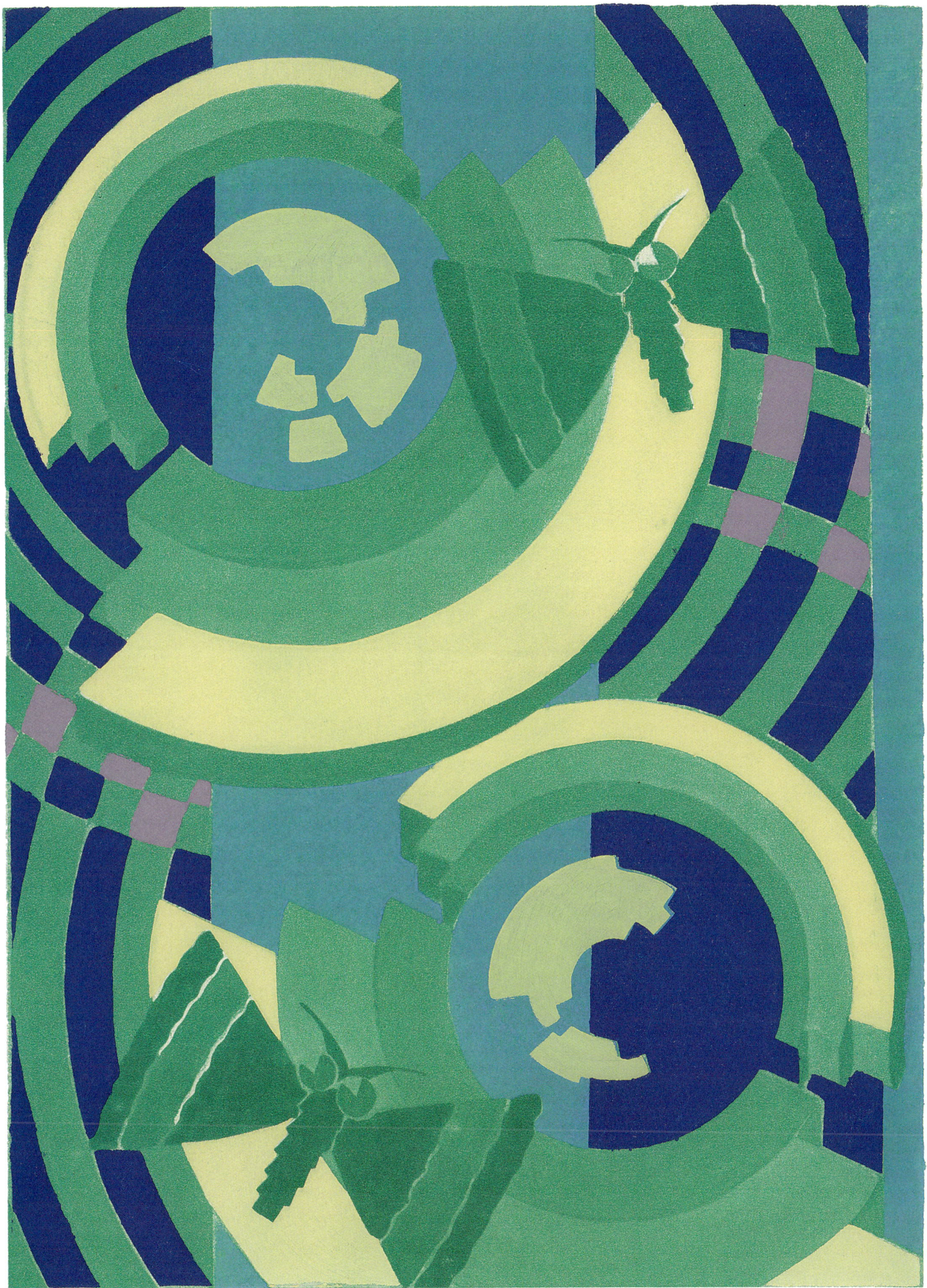

Plate 10

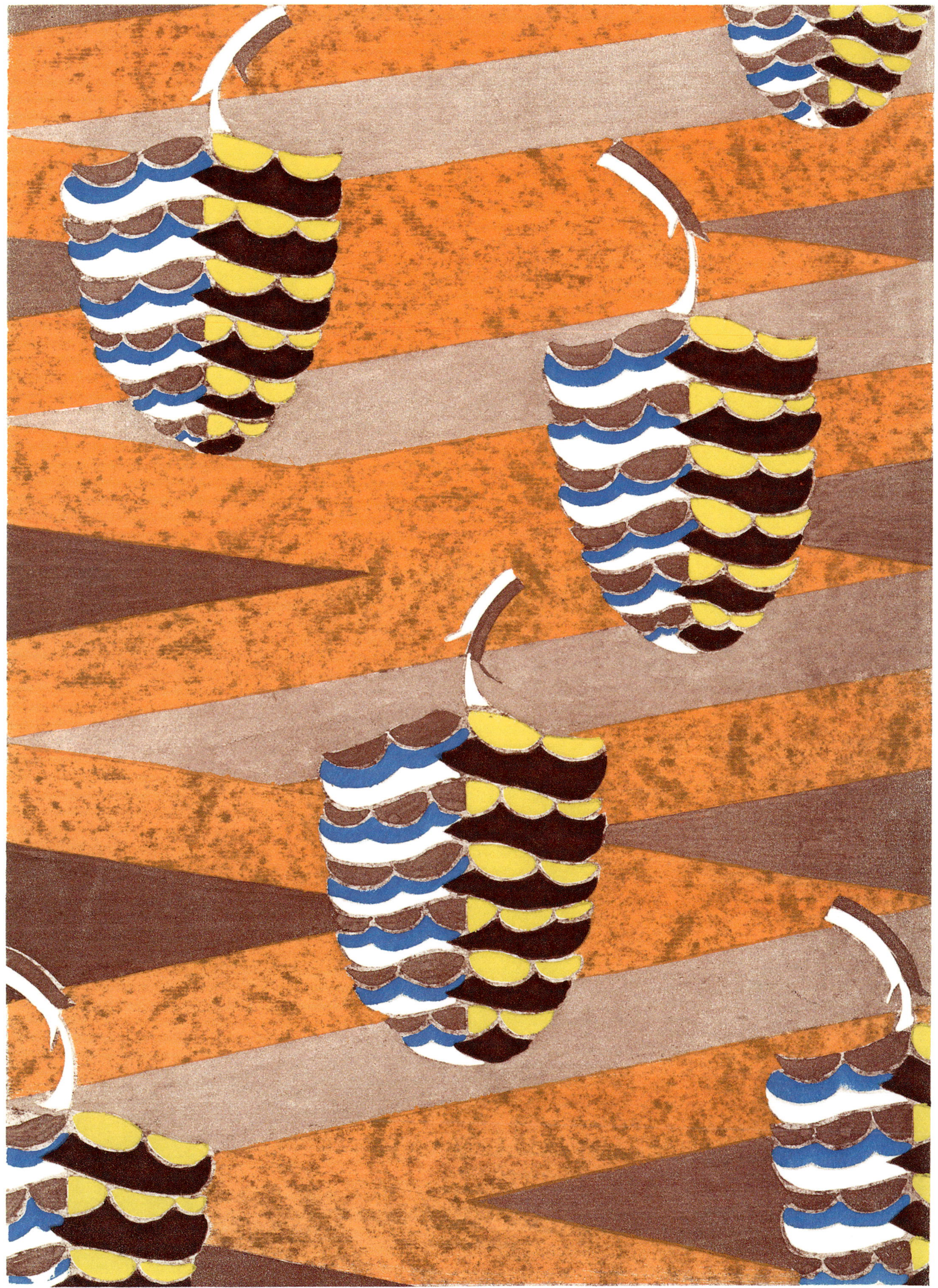

Plate 11

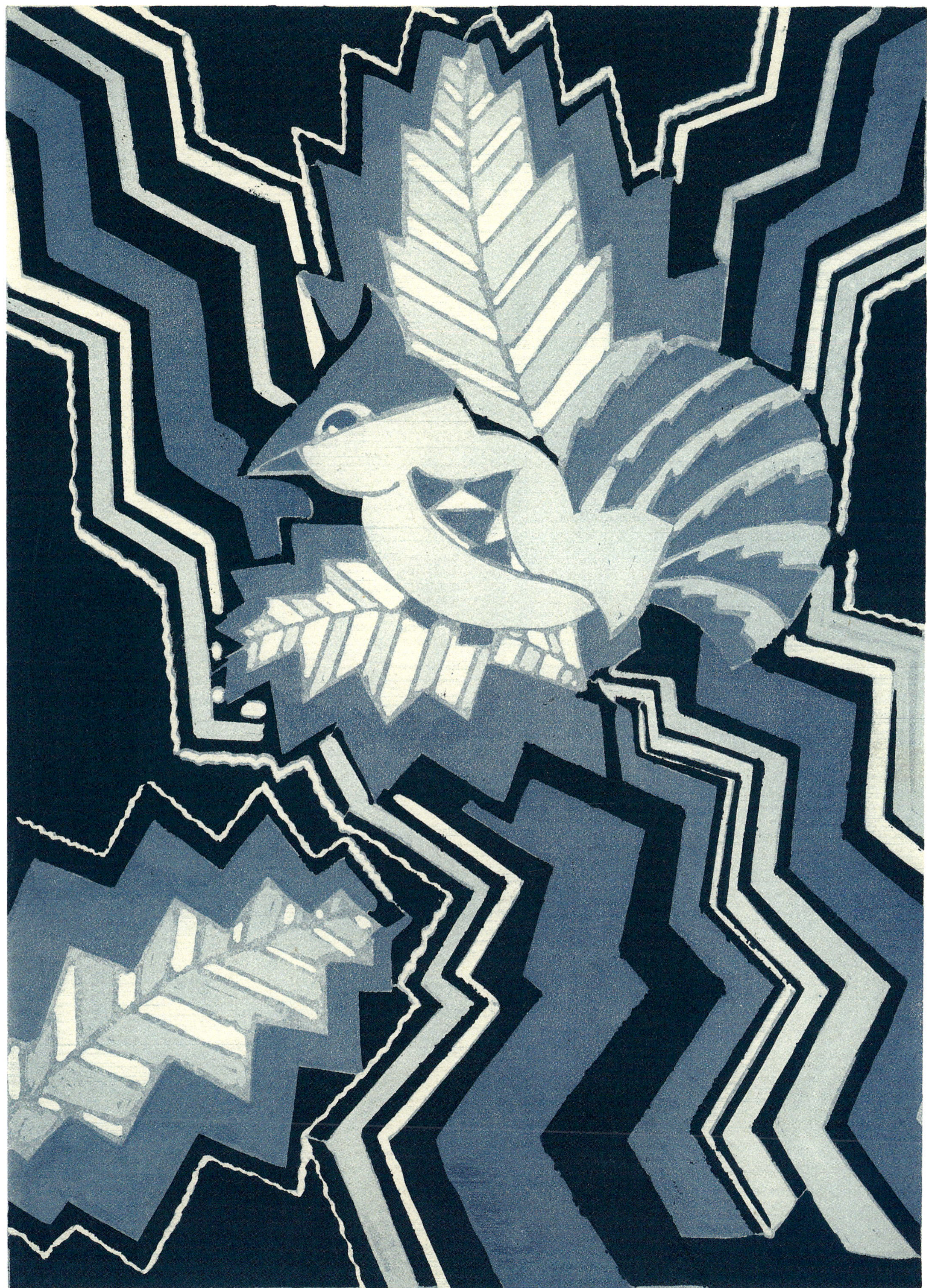

Plate 12

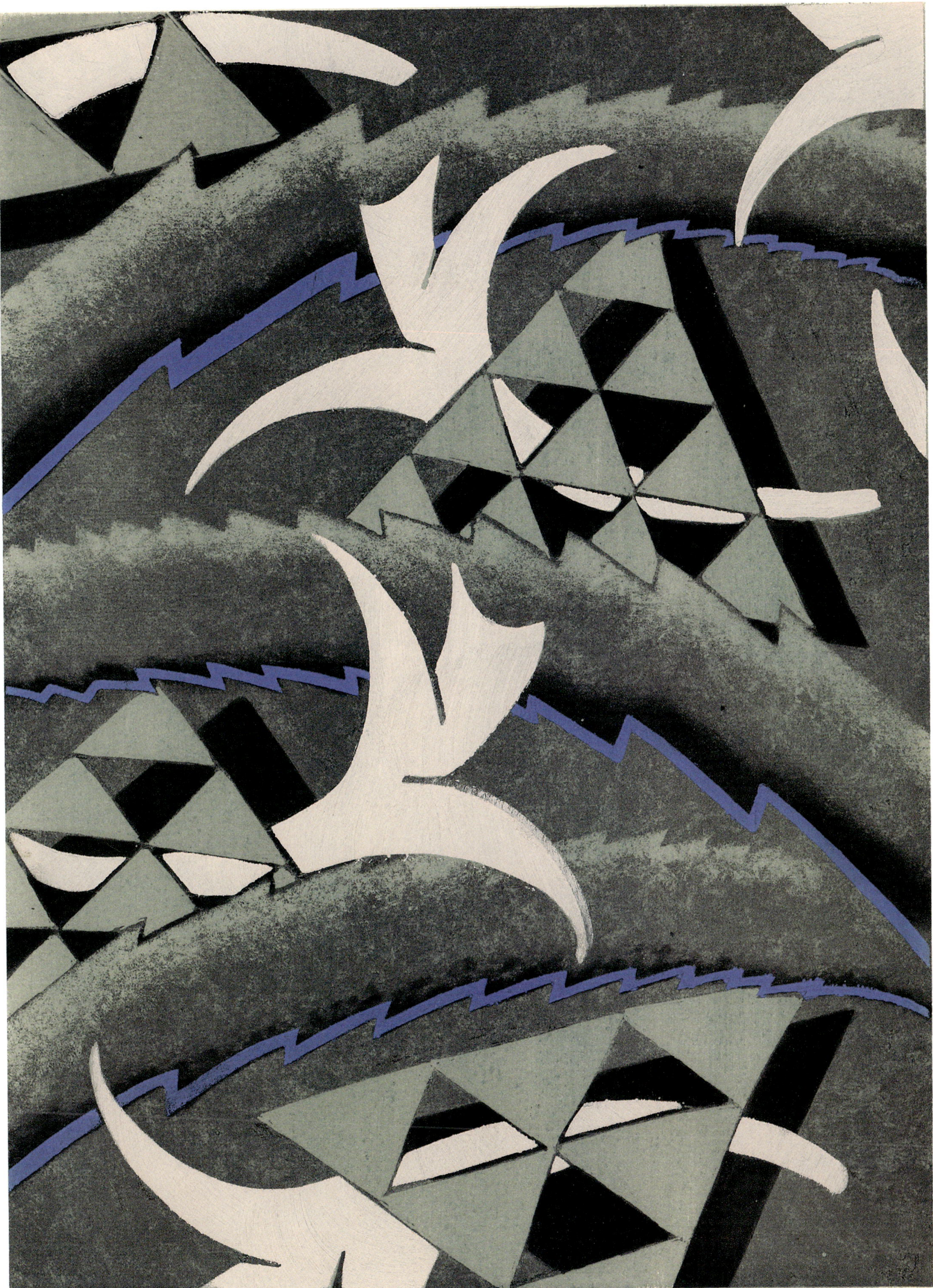

Plate 13

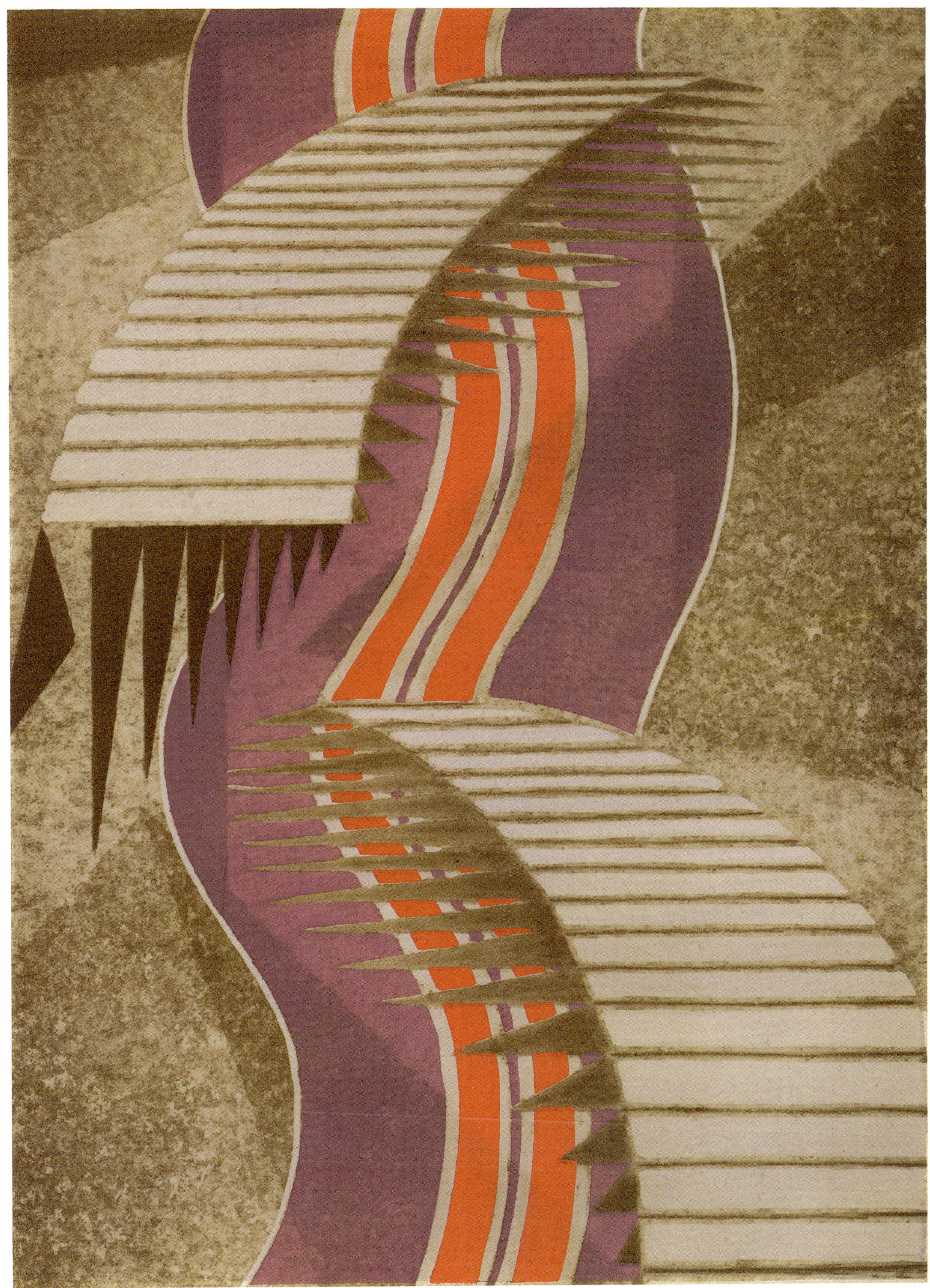

Plate 14

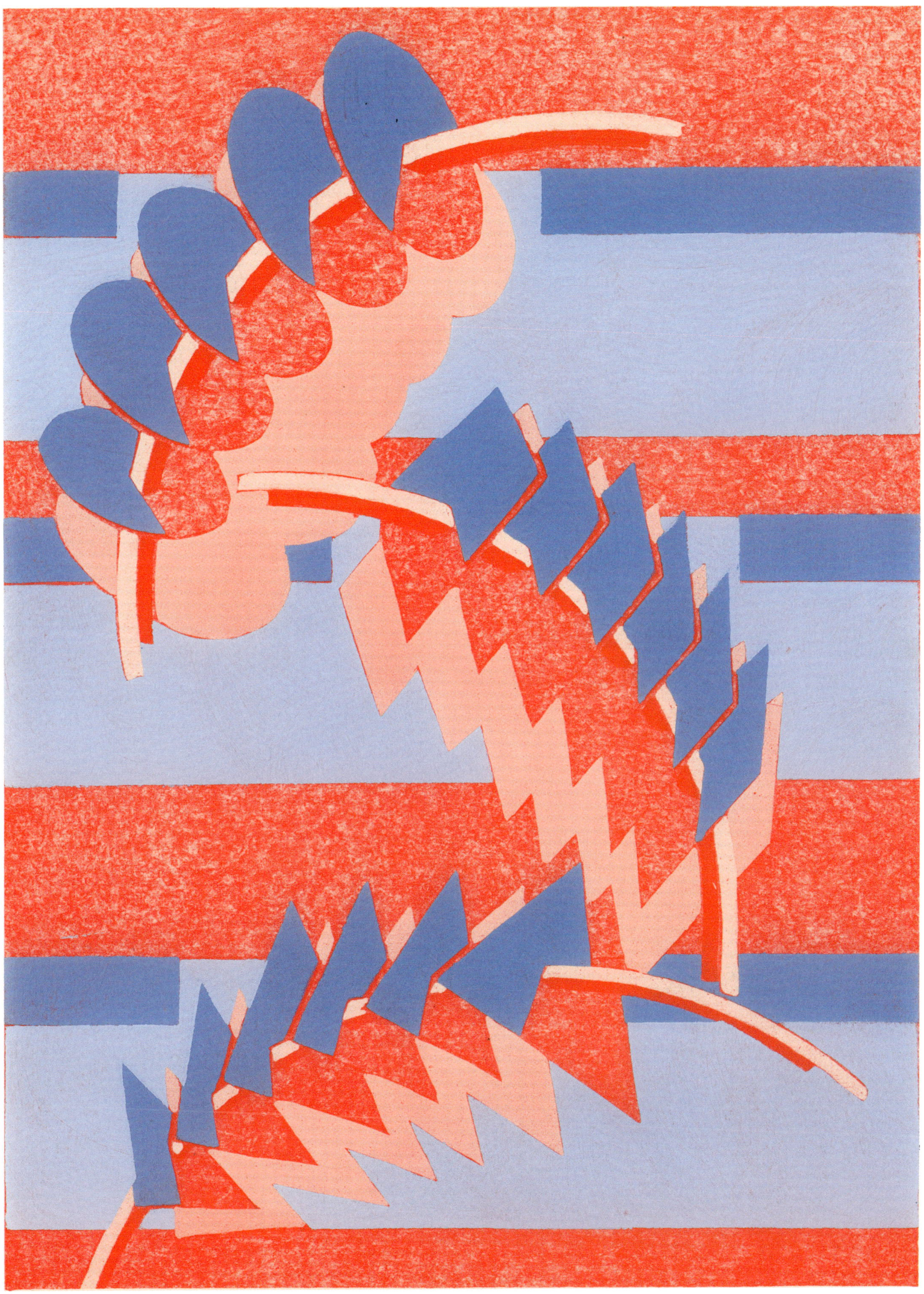

Plate 15

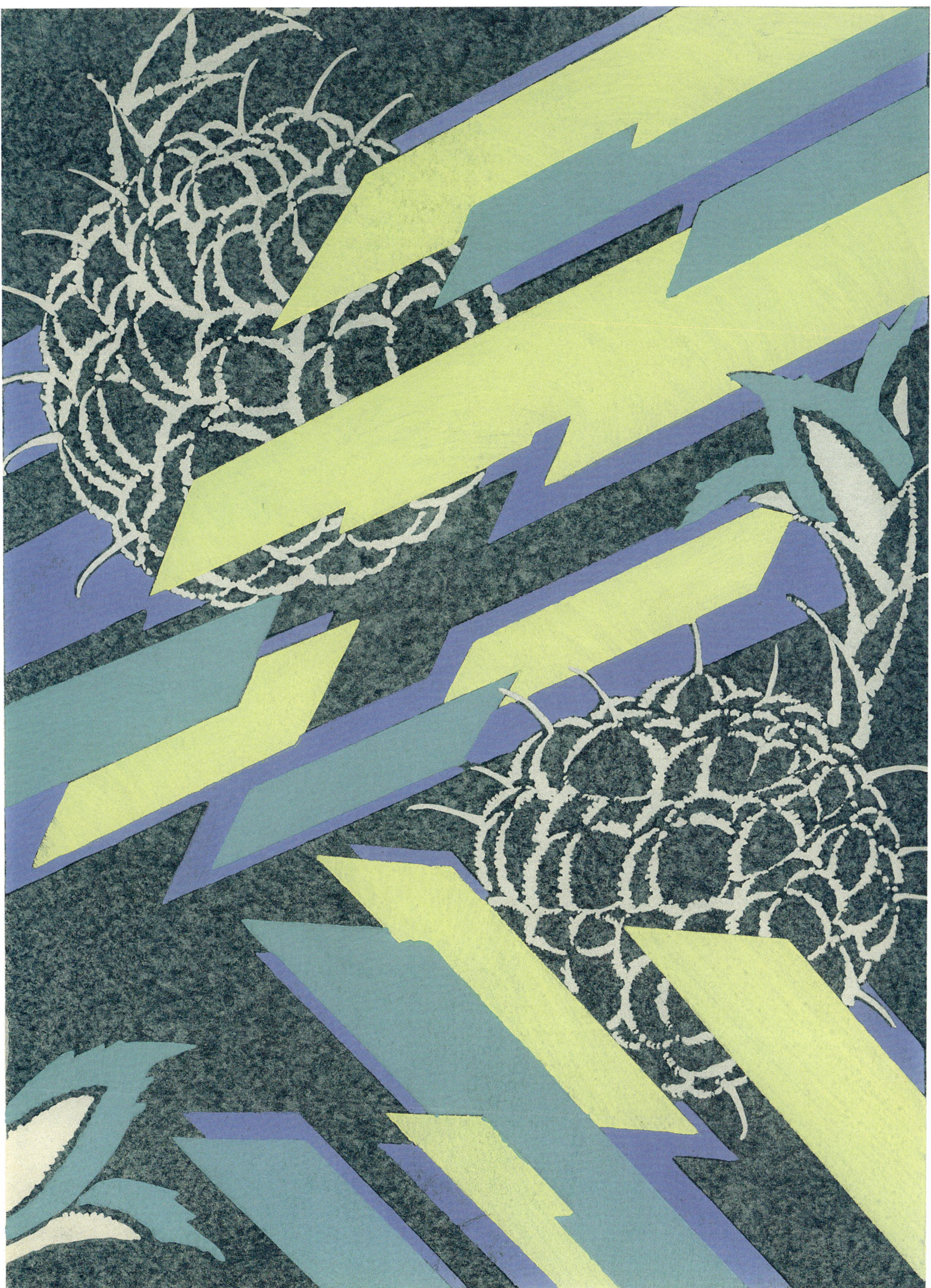

Plate 16

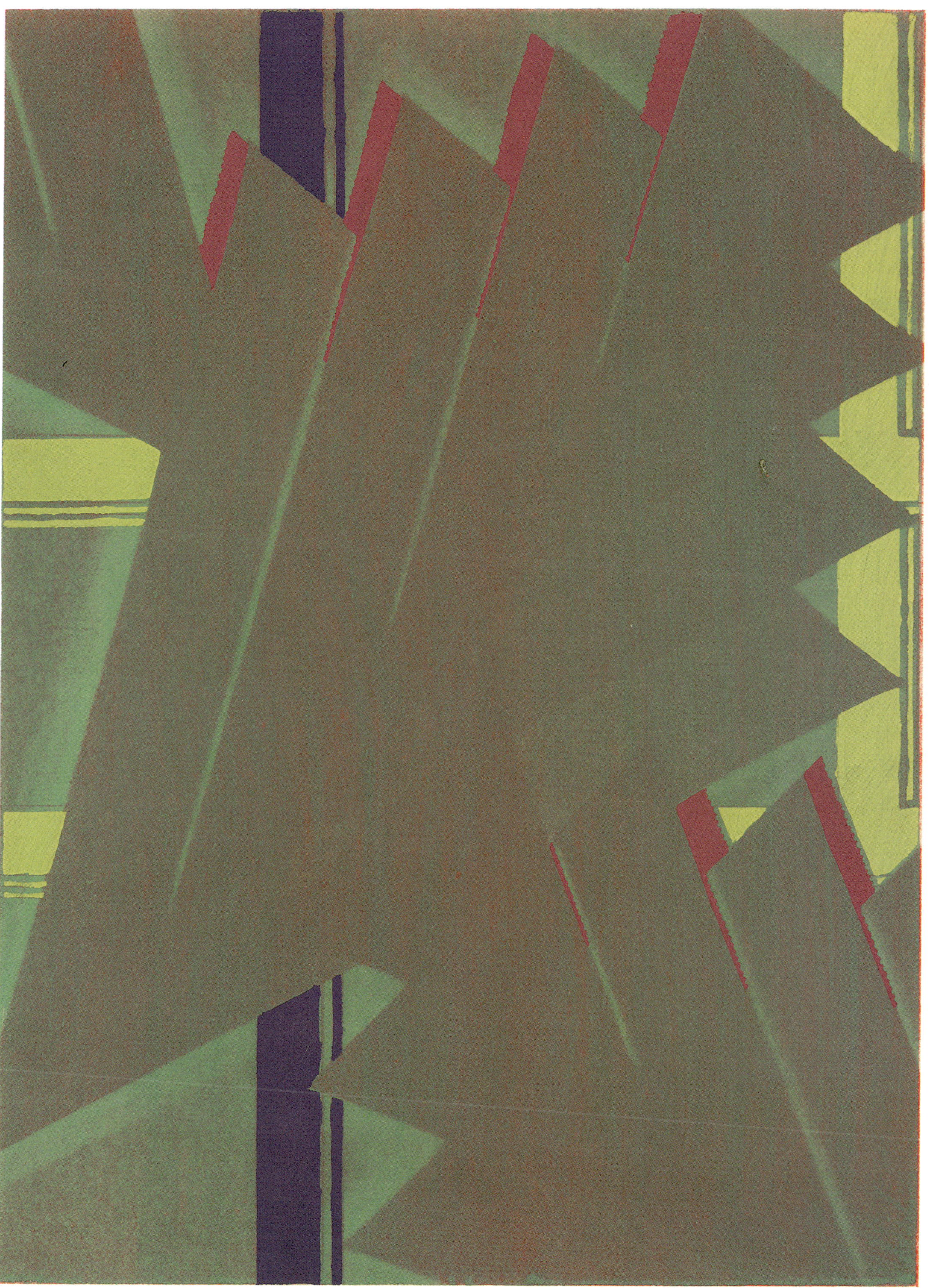

Plate 17

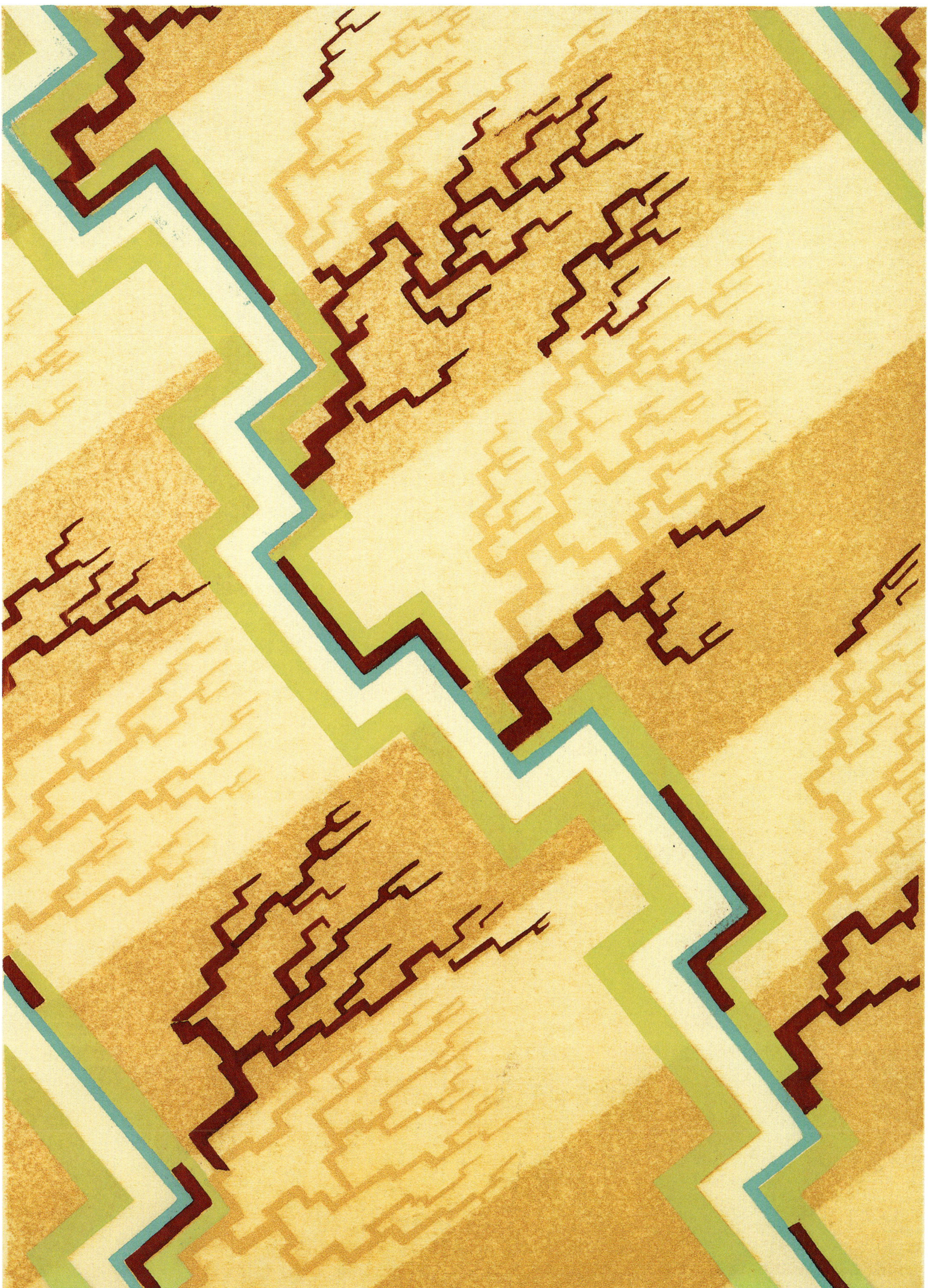

Plate 18

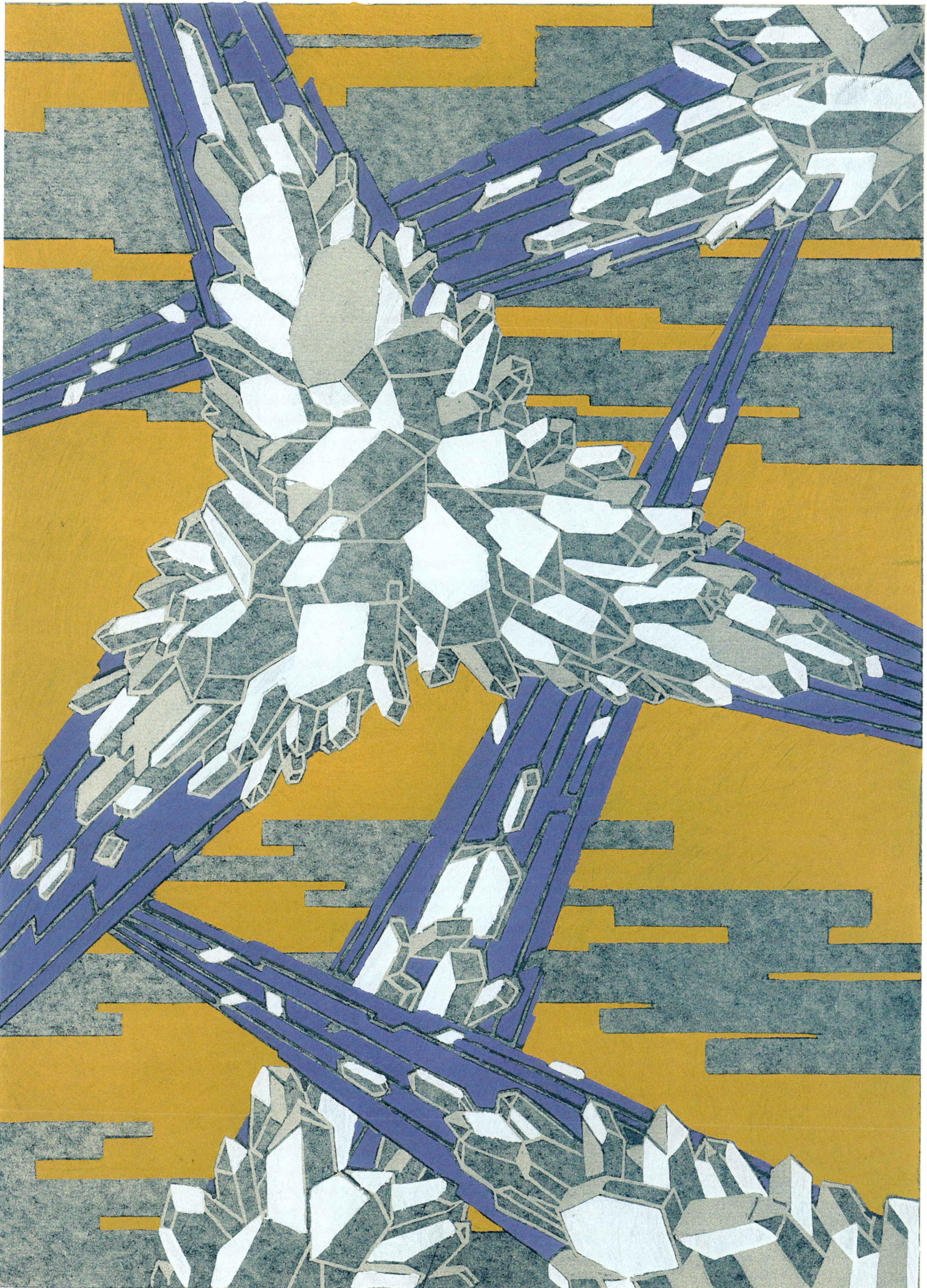

Plate 19

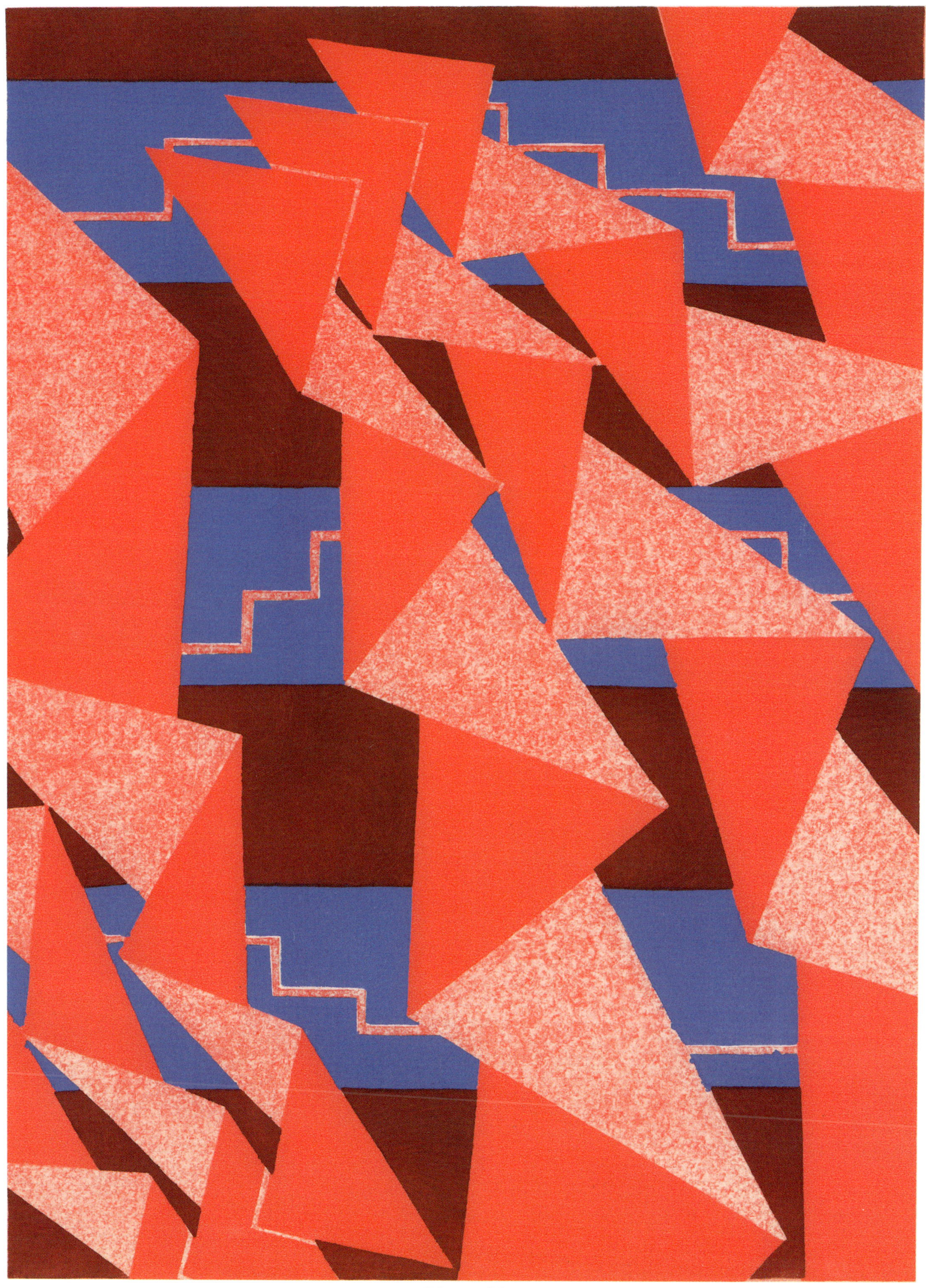

Plate 20

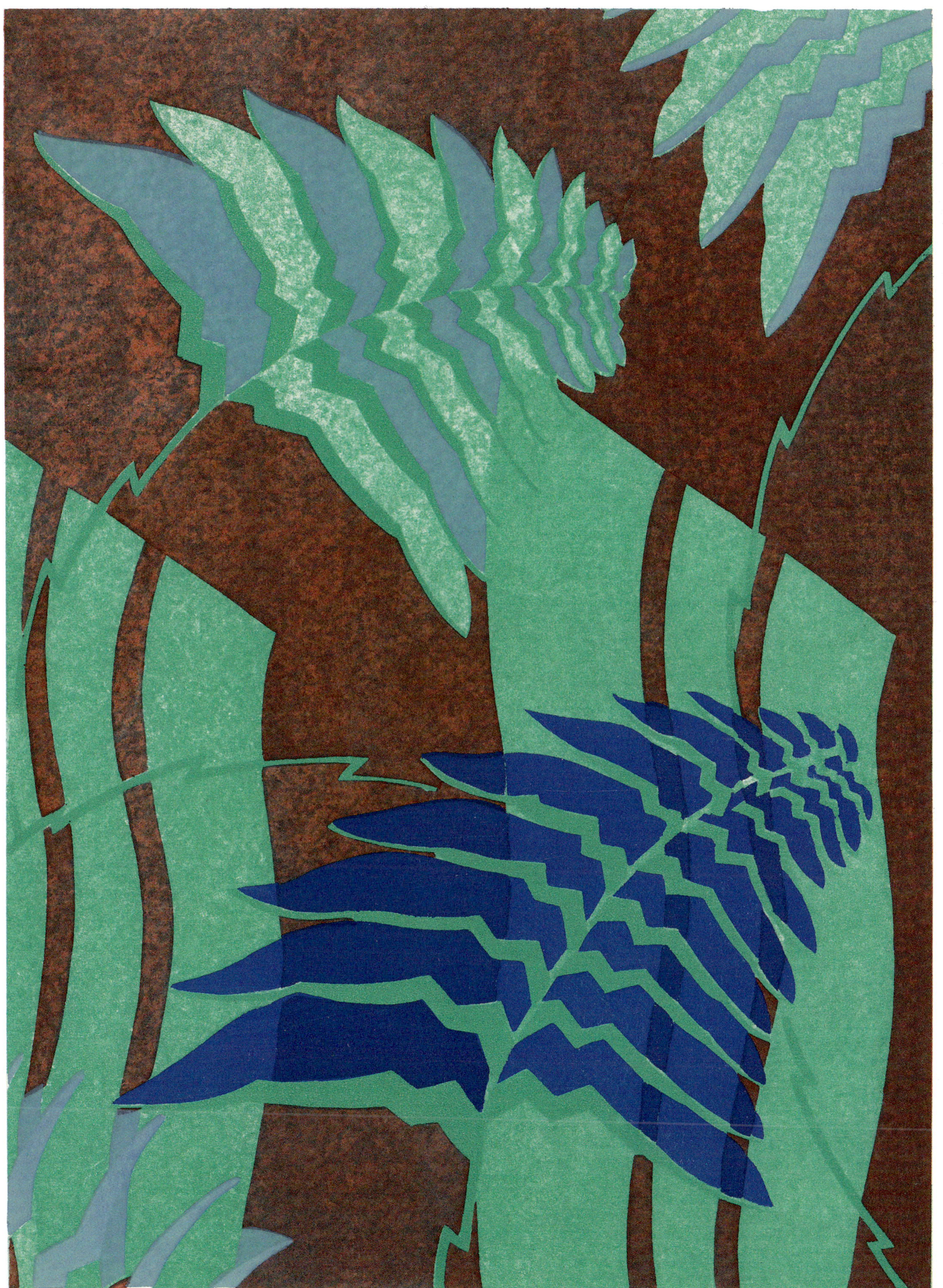

Plate 21

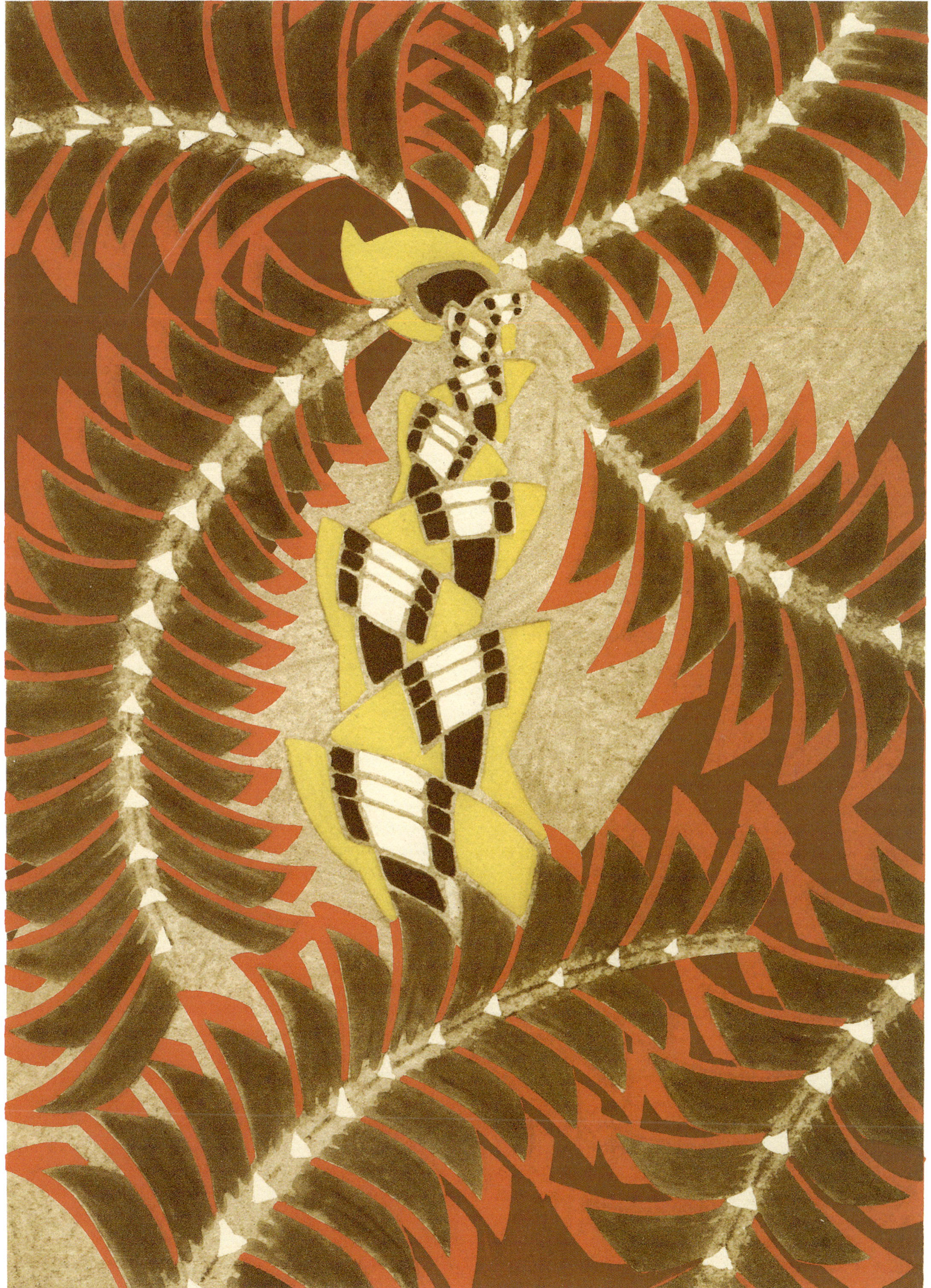

Plate 22

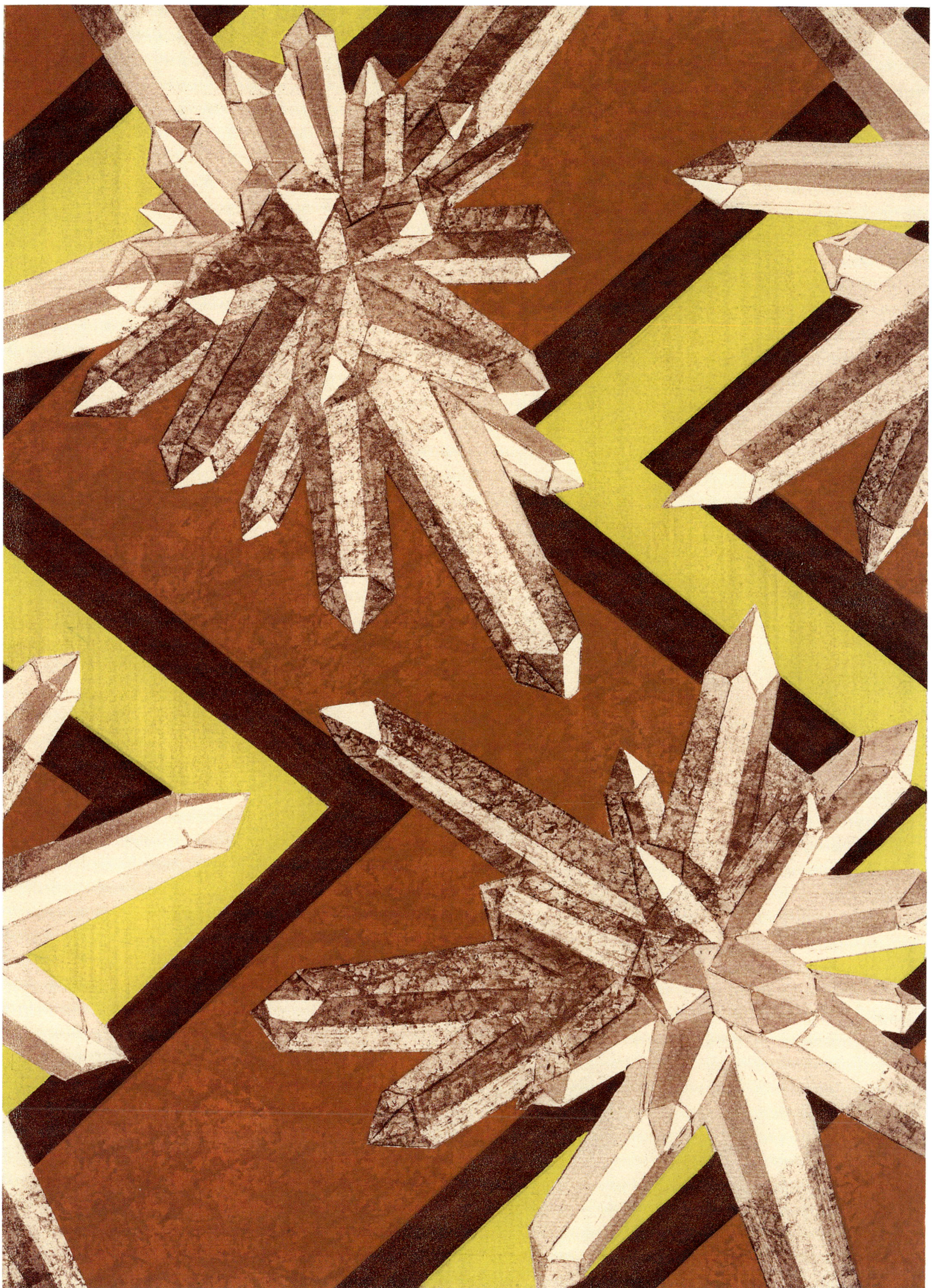

Plate 23

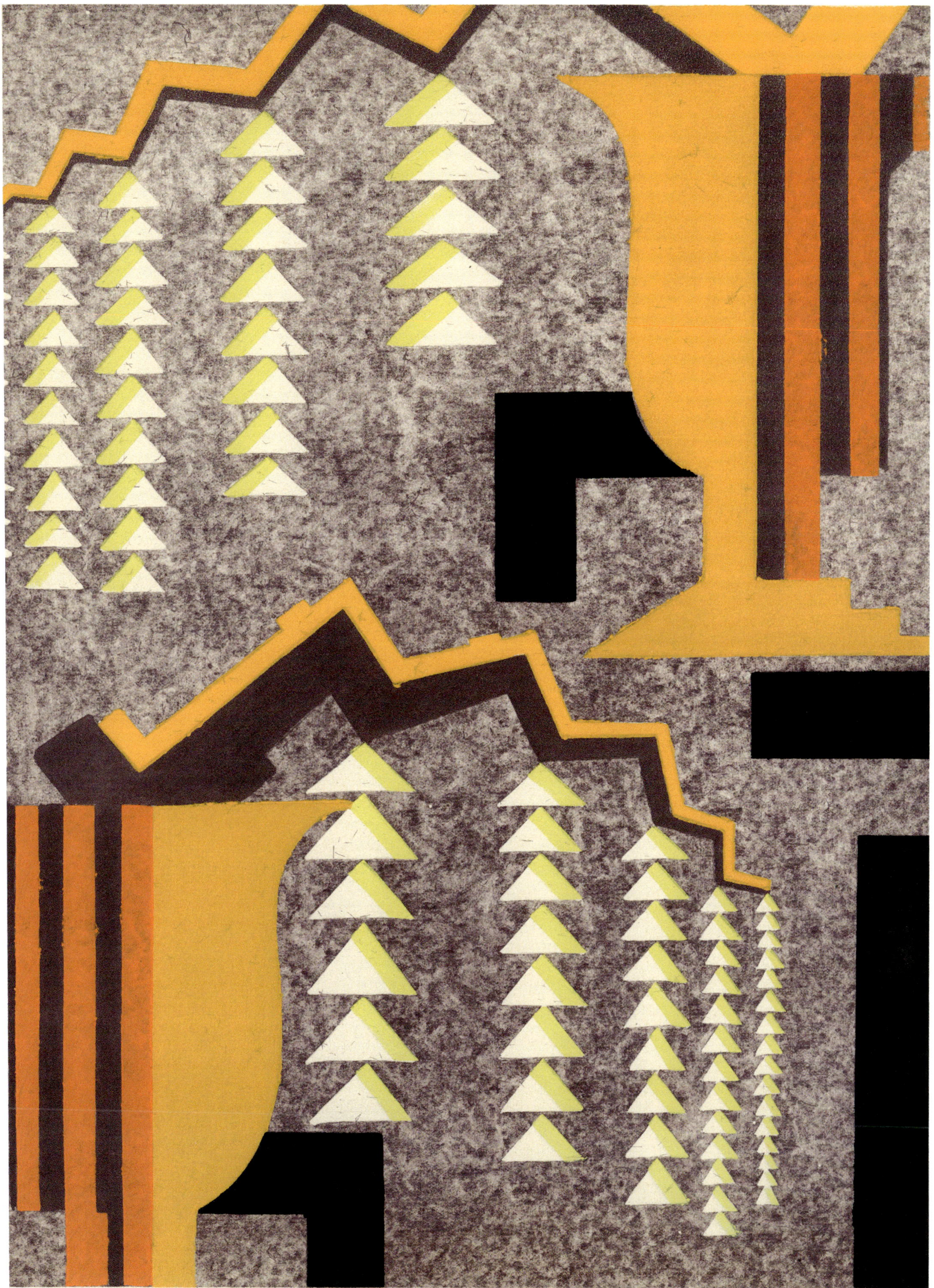

Plate 24

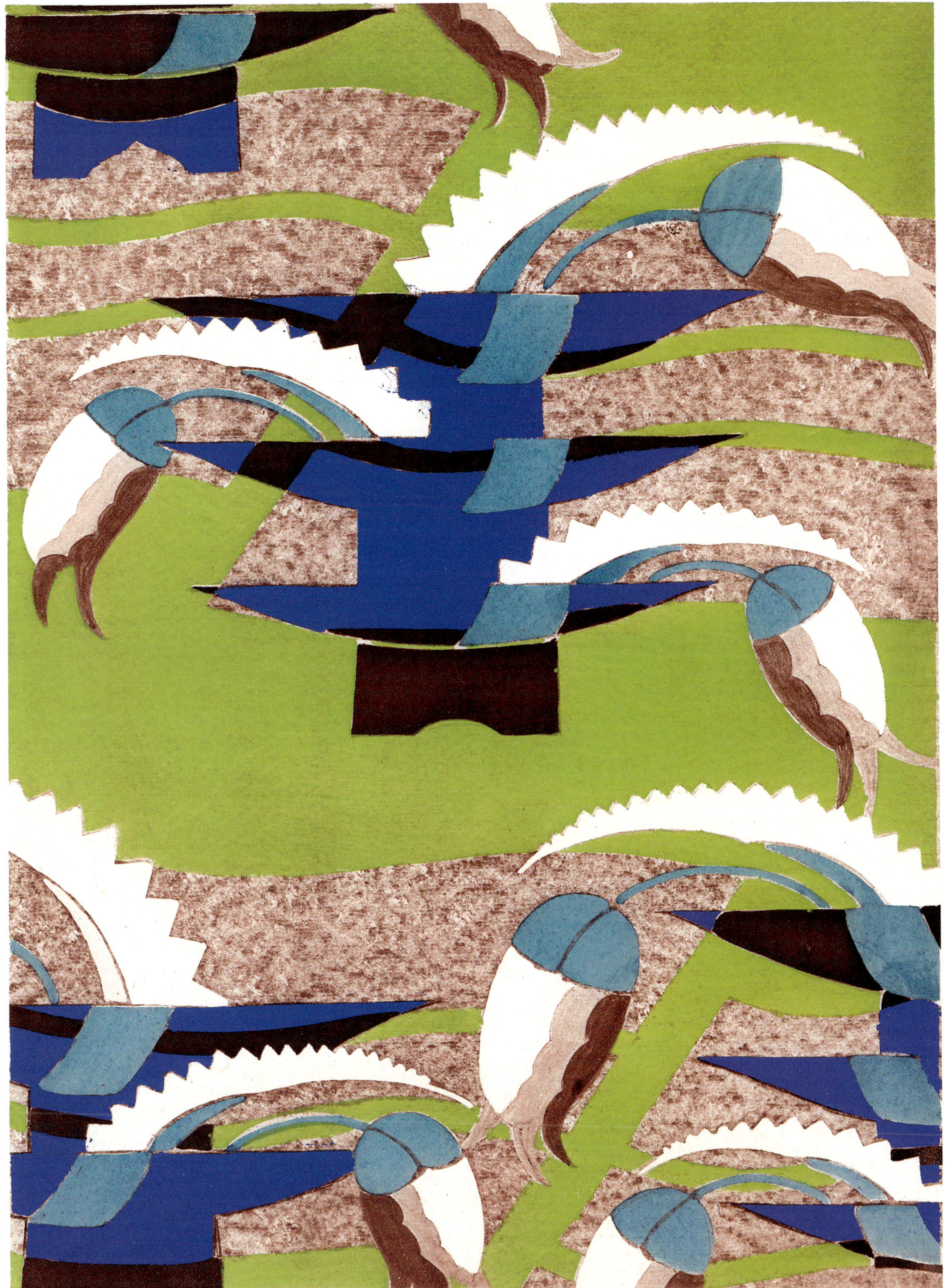

Plate 25

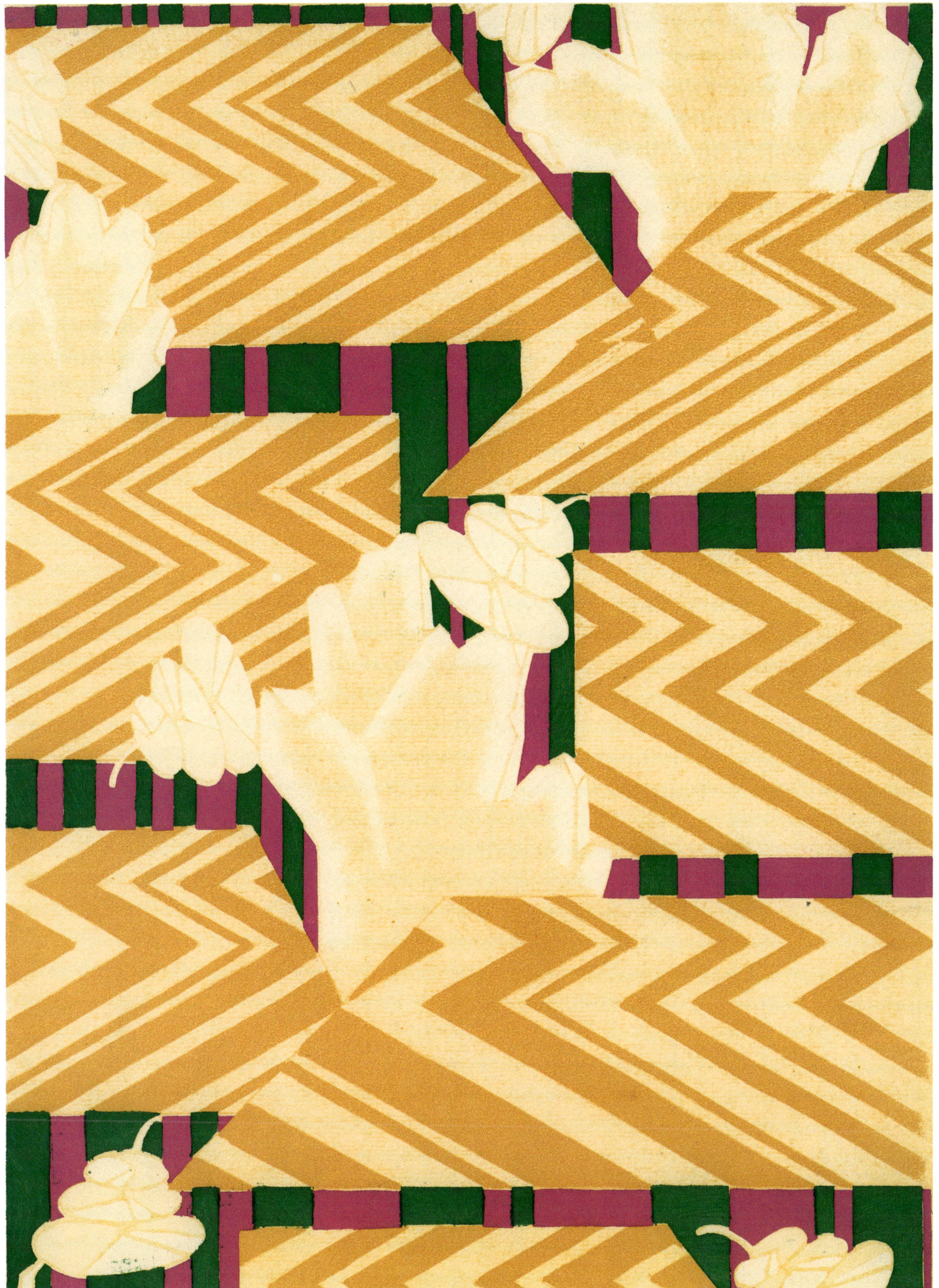

Plate 26

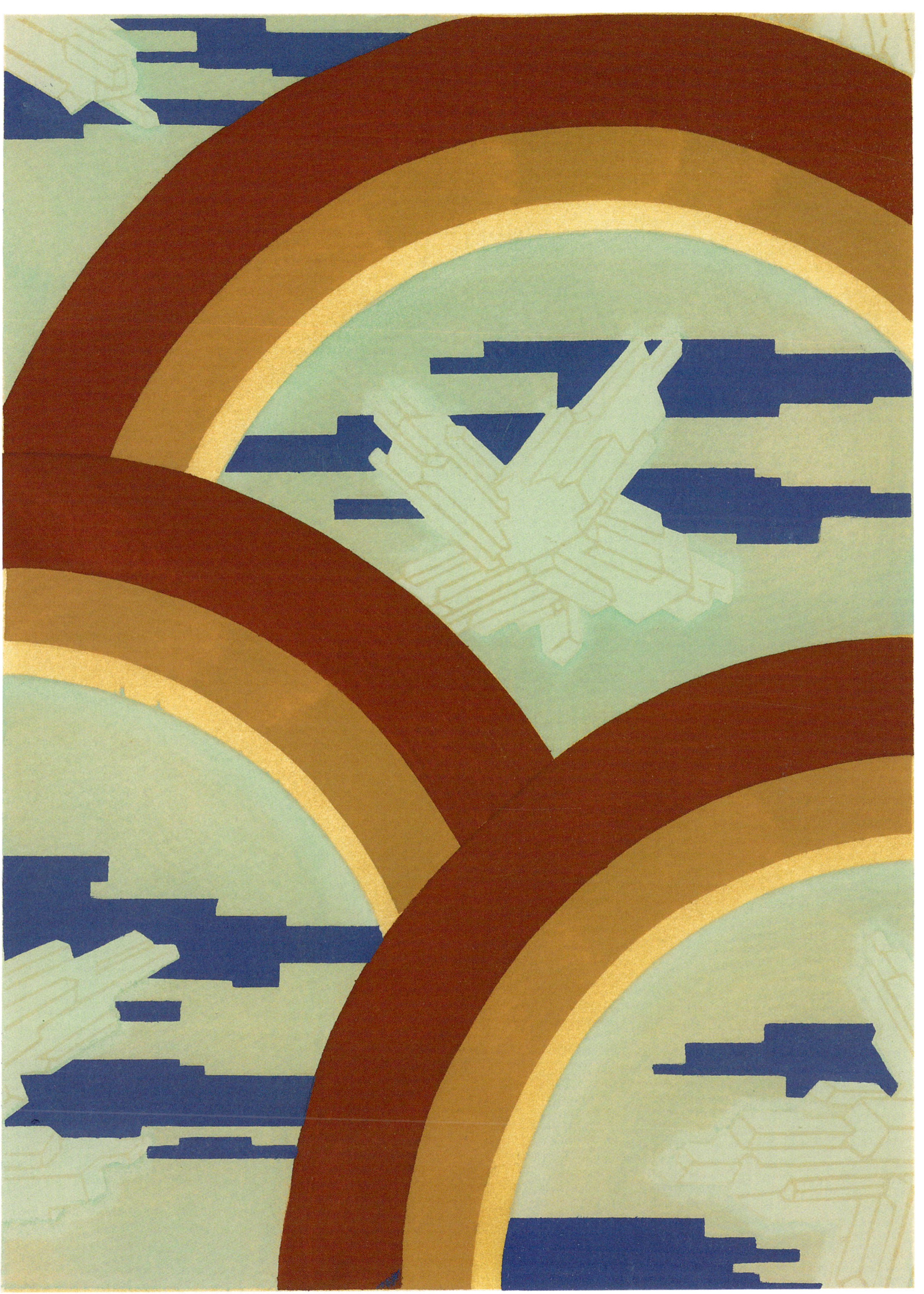

Plate 27

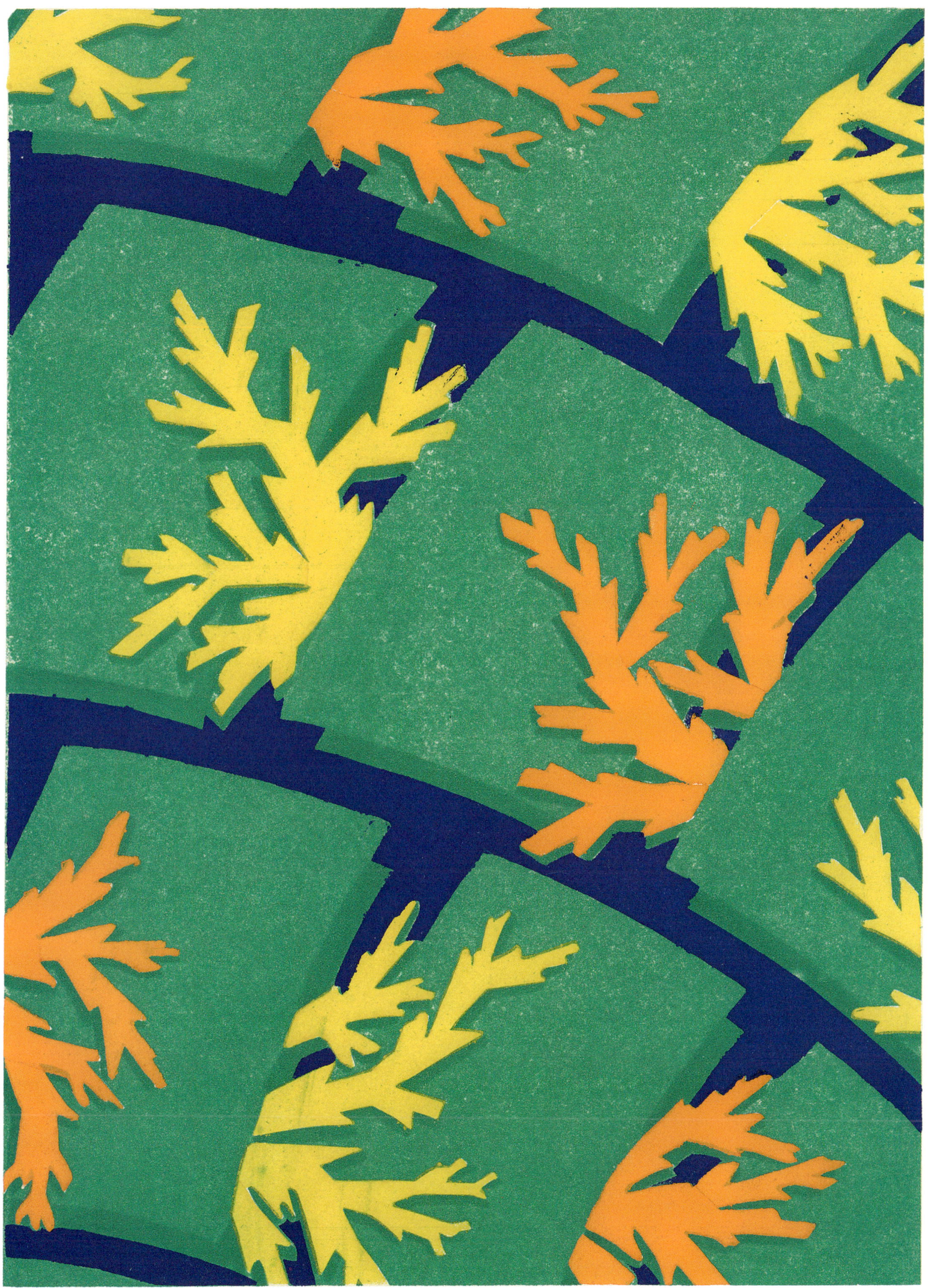

Plate 28

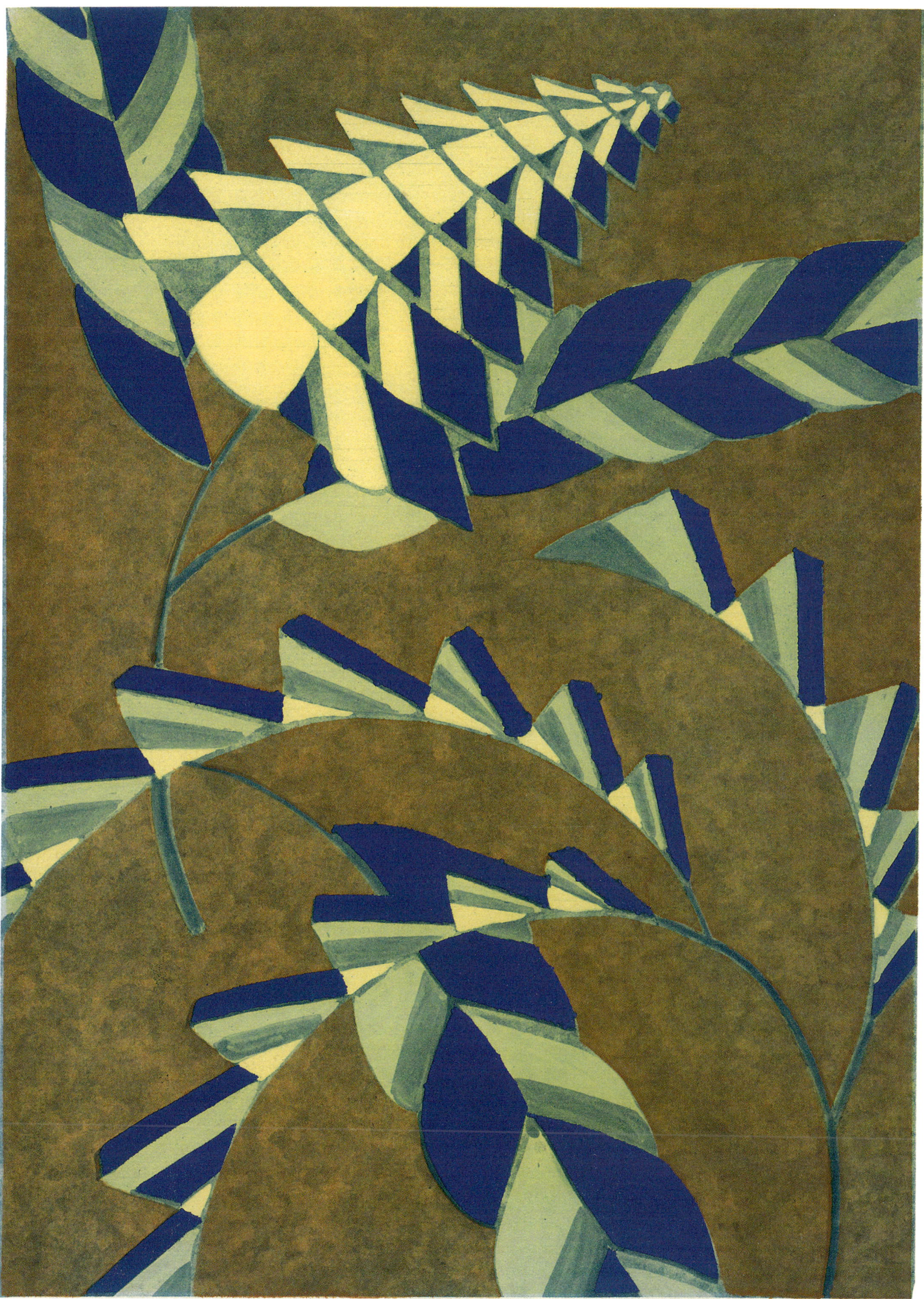

Plate 29

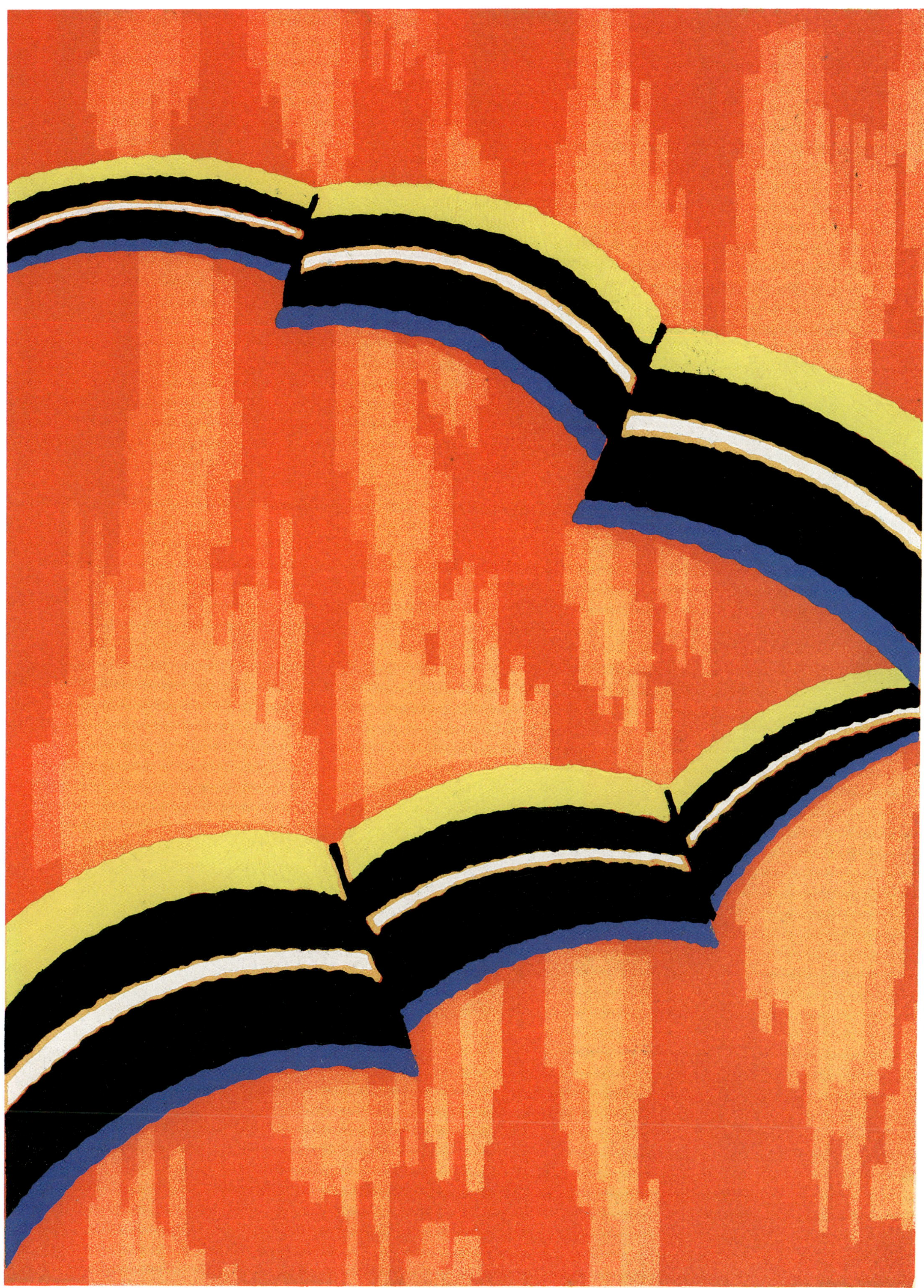

Plate 30

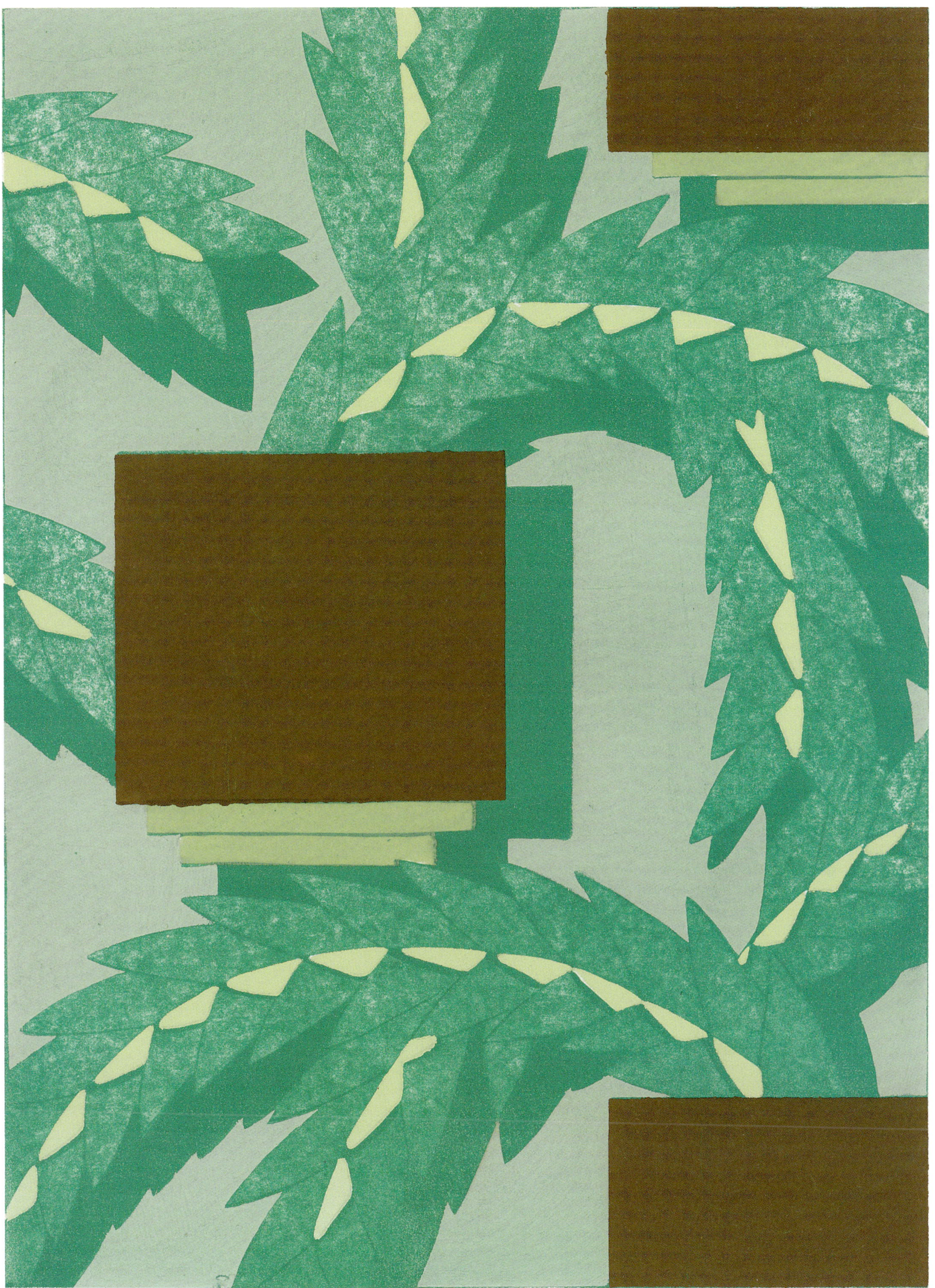

Plate 31

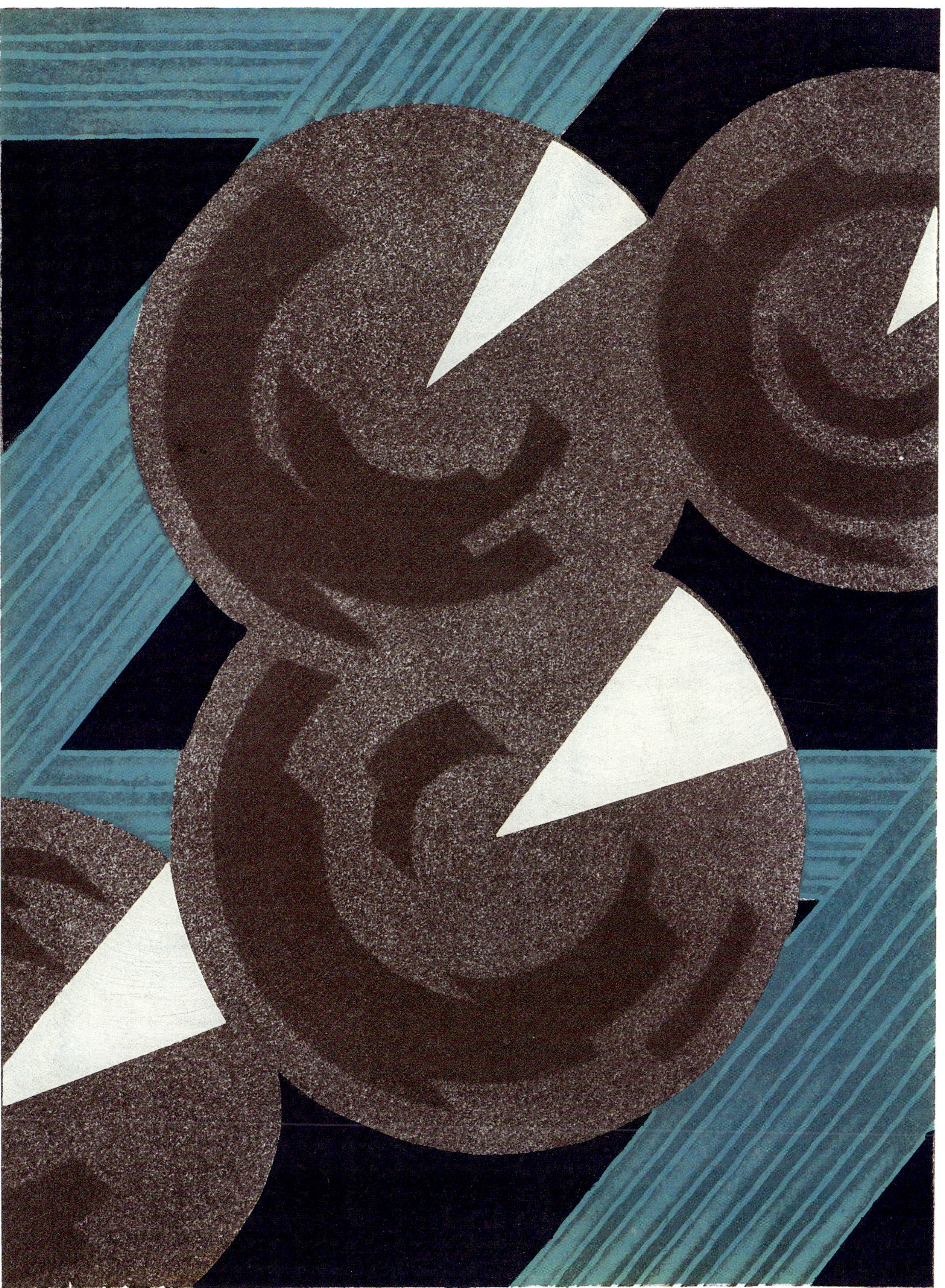

Plate 32

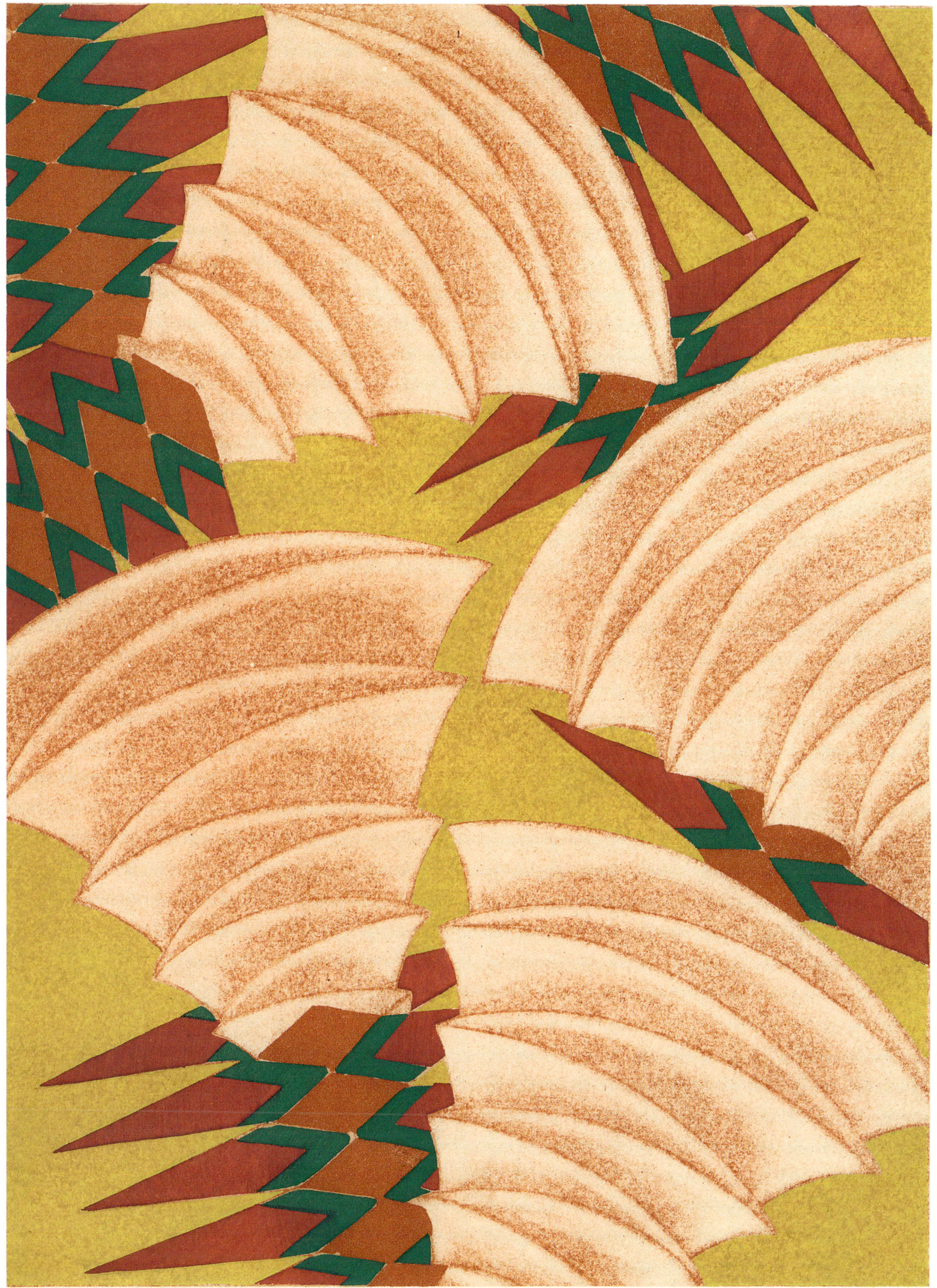

Plate 33

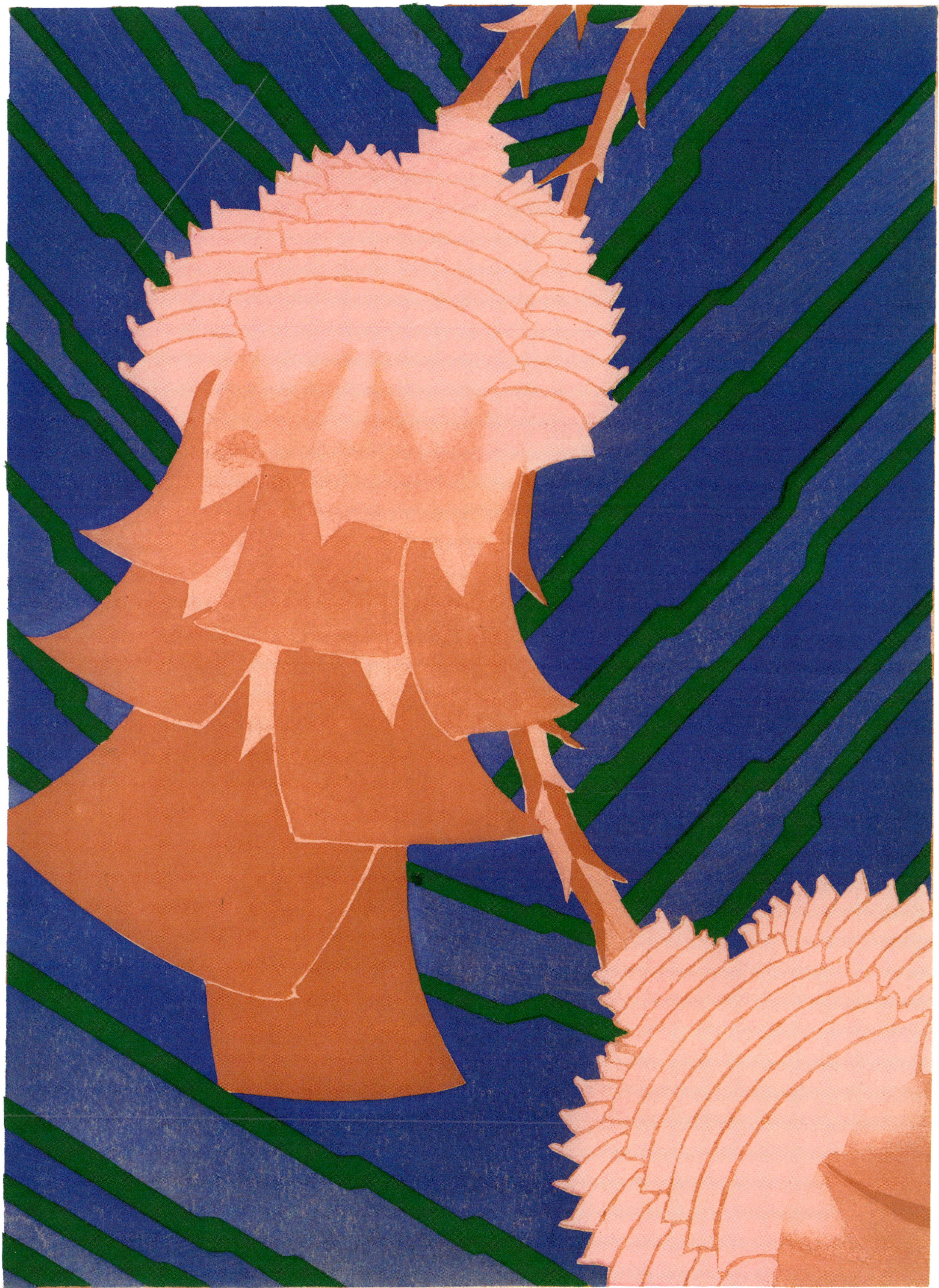

Plate 34

Plate 35

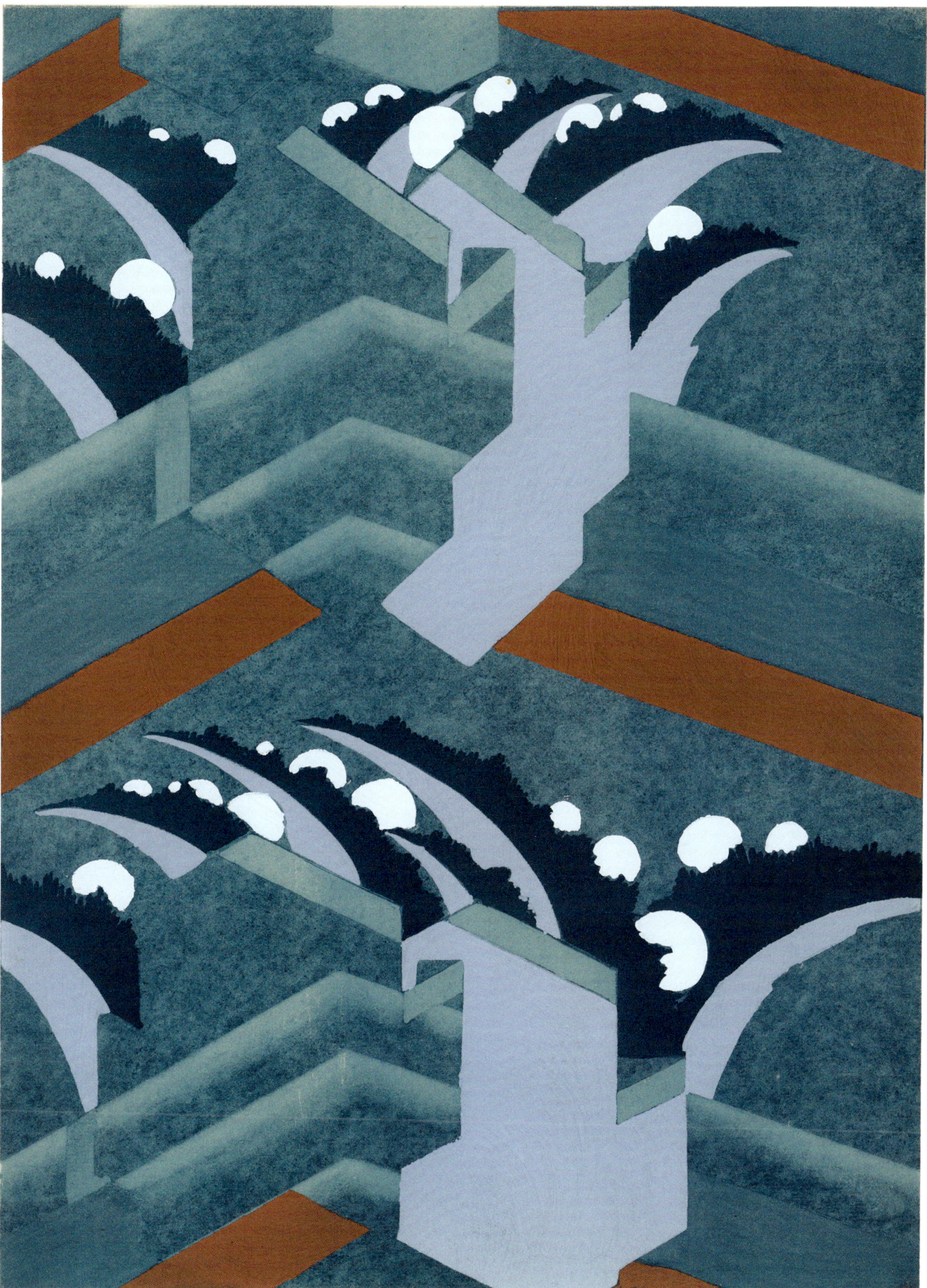

Plate 36

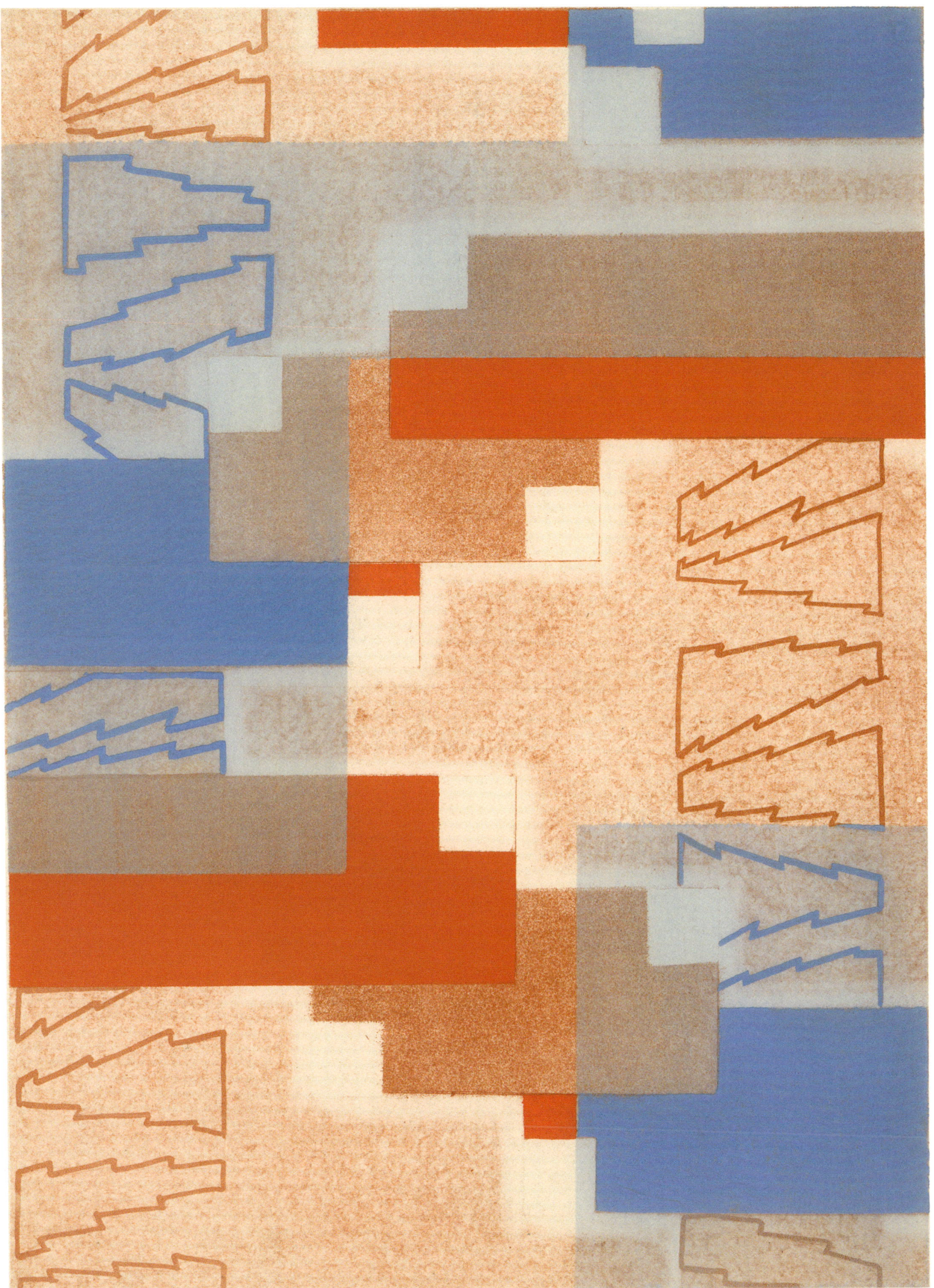

Plate 37

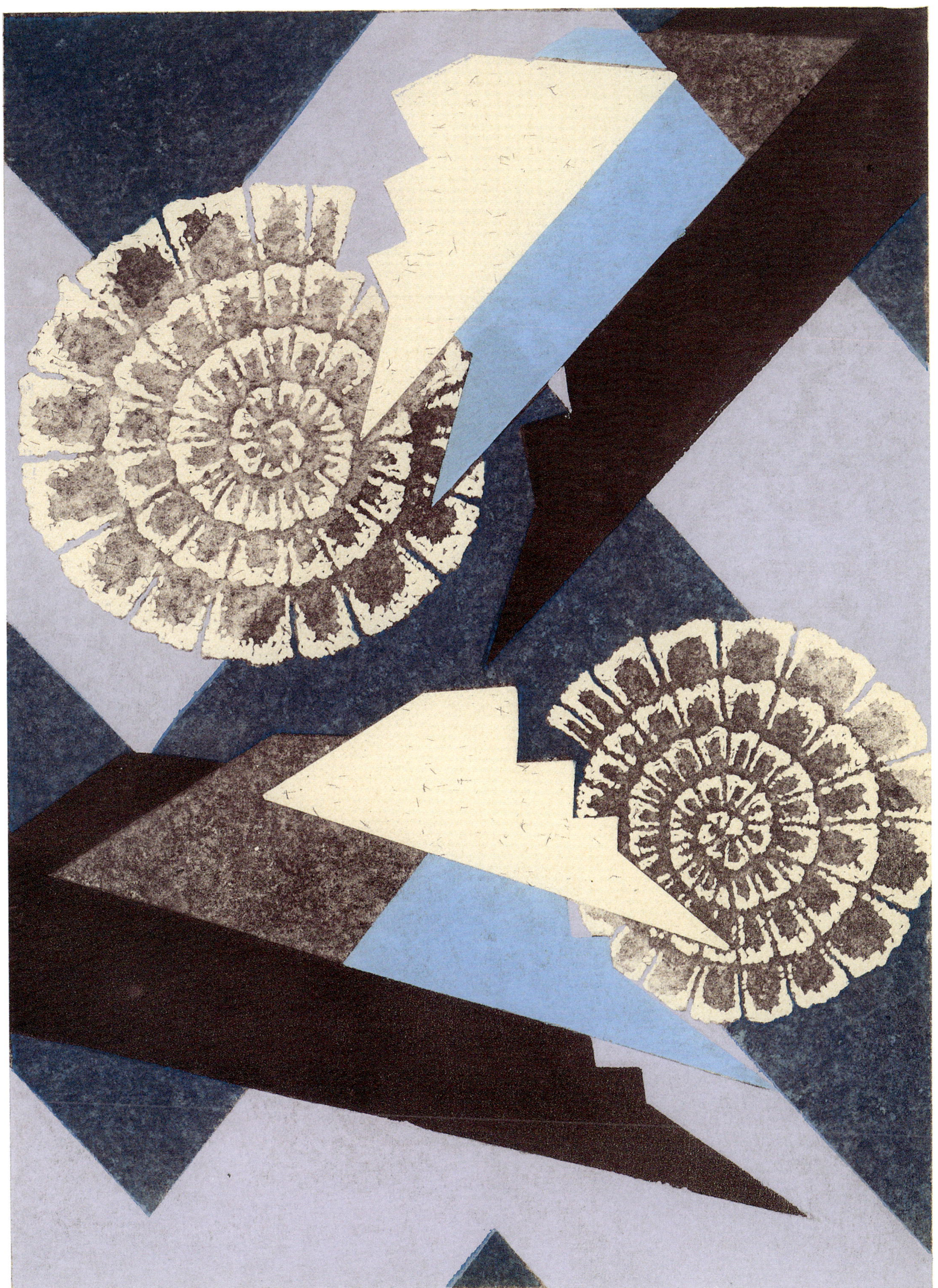

Plate 38

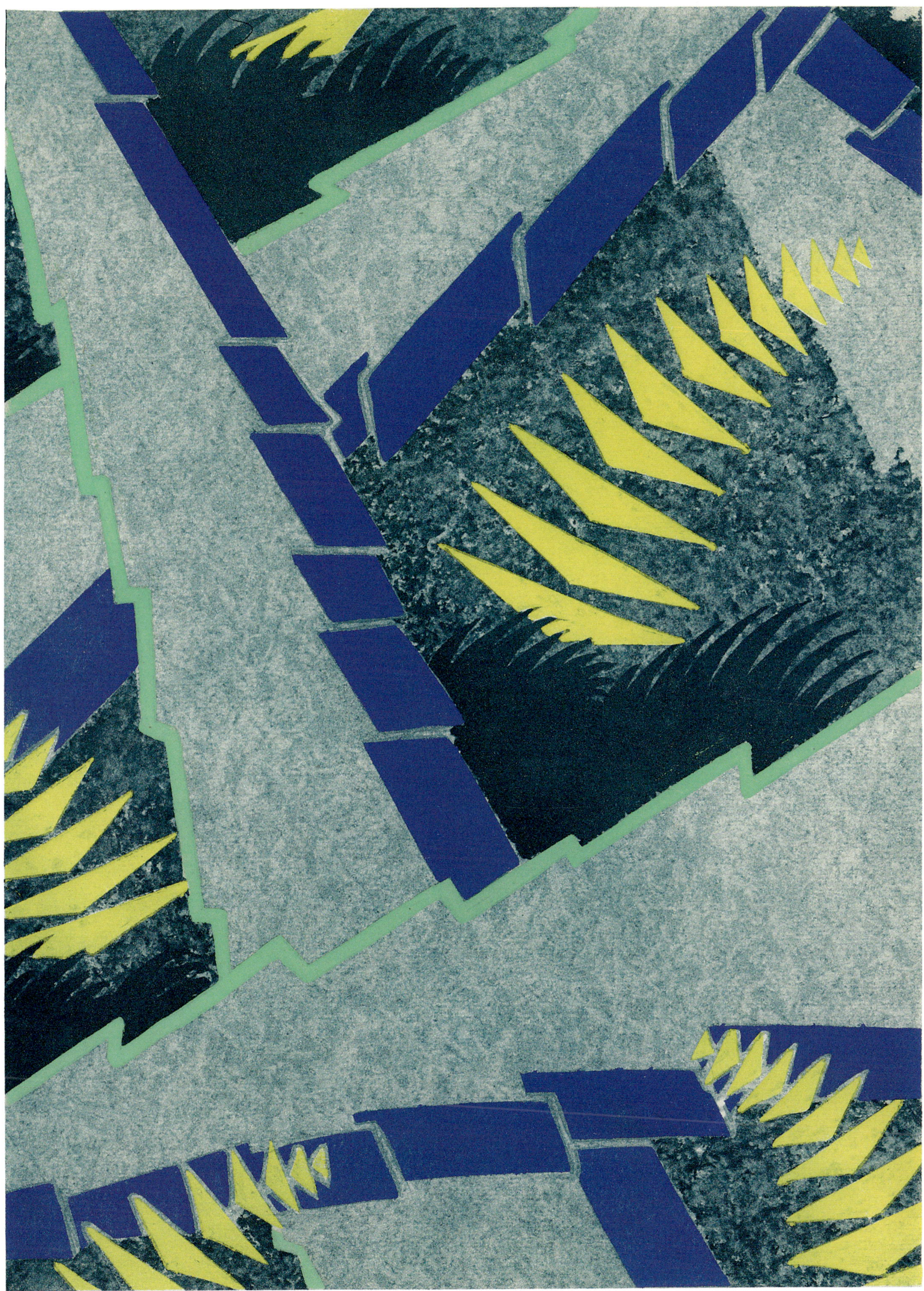

Plate 39

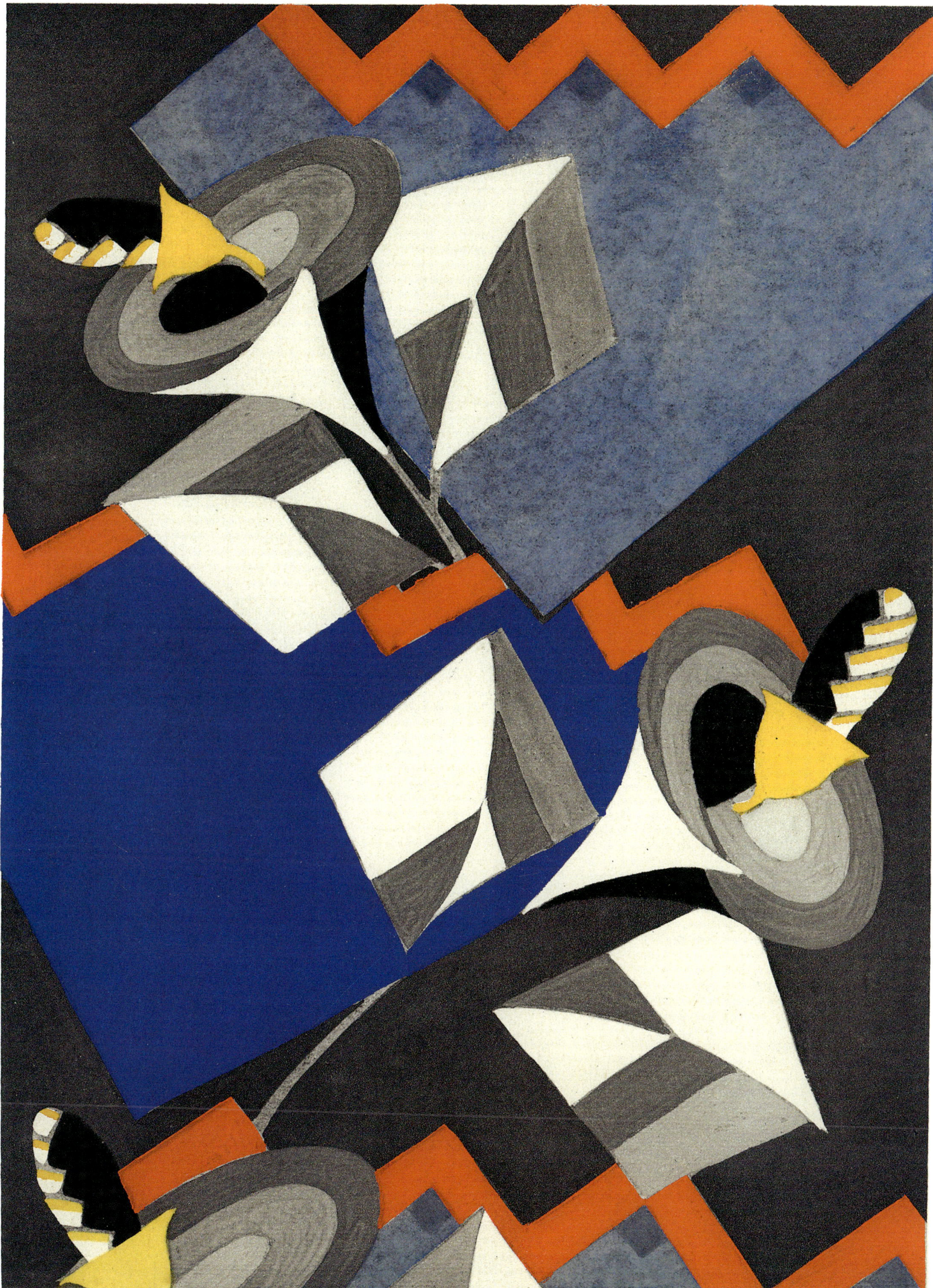

Plate 40